Of quills and swords.

Of power and betrayal.

Of a stage conquered and a throne lost!

Anonymous

WILLIAM SHAKESPEARE REVEALED

Introduction by ROLAND EMMERICH

Edited by **CHRISTOPHER MEASOM**　　Designed by **TIMOTHY SHANER**

A Newmarket Pictorial Moviebook

Newmarket Press

Contents

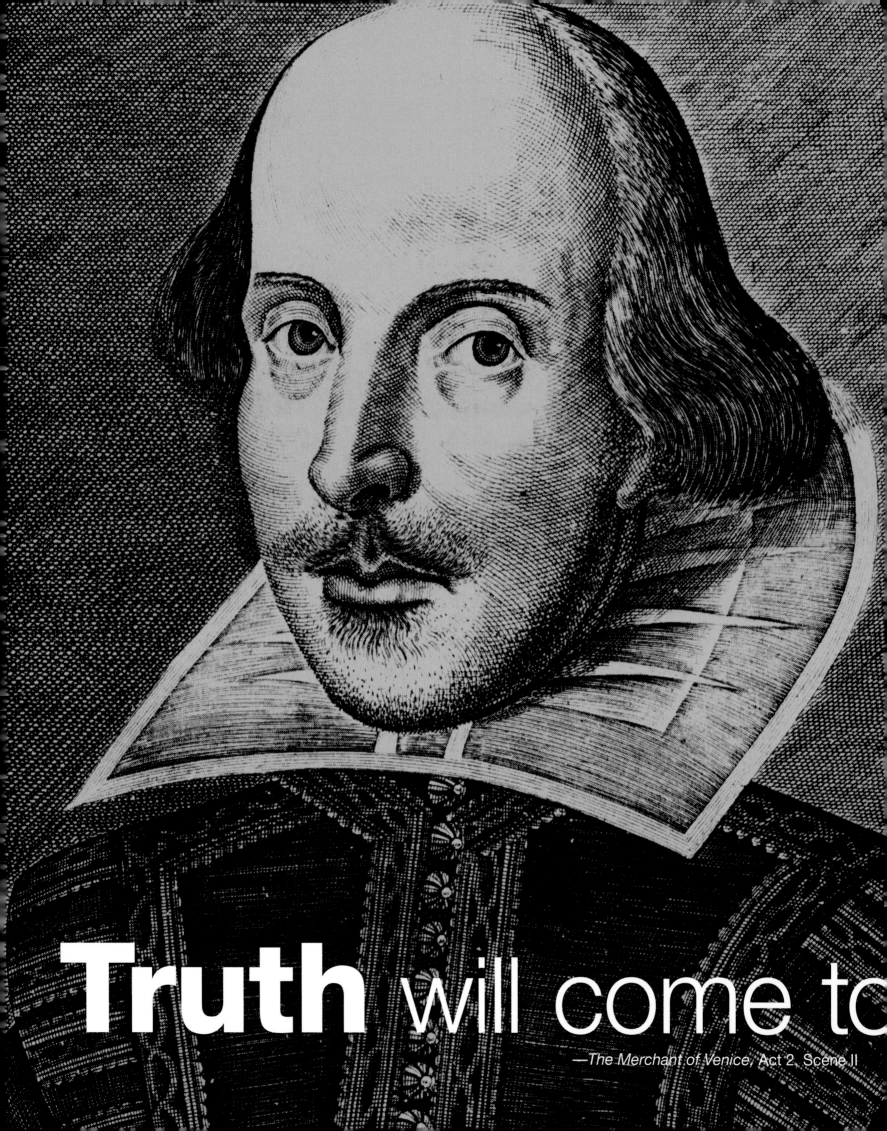

Truth will come to

—*The Merchant of Venice, Act 2, Scene II*

A Shakespearean
CONSPIRACY

Roland Emmerich

I am ruined.

As I am writing this, I am preparing for the first official screening of *Anonymous* and I am filled with longing to return to this set. A desire, if you will, to re-create what has been the single greatest filmmaking experience of my life.

What sets this production apart from the dozens of others I have produced or directed? To be honest, it is not something, I feel, I can express in words. But for the sake of this introduction, I will try.

Before there was a cast, before there were sets and costumes, there was the script. I came across this story while looking for a writer to work with me on the script for *The Day After Tomorrow*. I was given John Orloff's "The Soul of the Age," a script that suggested that somebody else was the true author of Shakespeare's collected works.

I had heard rumors about this idea before, and John's script made a plausible, yet fictional, story out of it. Quite daring, I might say, and I was immediately attracted to it. When I did my own research, I soon found out that there are quite a few different theories circulating about the true authorship of Shakespeare, and I realized that I had stumbled upon a topic of great controversy.

I optioned the script, and John and

I went to work on a rewrite. I always felt that the script had great emotional heart, but lacked an overall theme. John and I kicked around a lot of ideas but I didn't want the movie to only be about the fact that Shakespeare was not the true author. I felt the story should be about something more and, like in some of the Bard's best plays, it had to be a tragedy. So John and I asked ourselves, "What was the single most important fact of Queen Elizabeth's world towards the end of her reign?" The conclusion was an easy one: Succession! Most of her court was scheming who would be the successor to the "Virgin Queen." With this, we had found the plot and the theme of our story. In

OPPOSITE: *Engraving of William Shakespeare by Martin Droeshout from the First Folio, 1623.* ABOVE: *Director Roland Emmerich on the bear-baiting set.*

7

Hamlet, Shakespeare writes, "Many wearing rapiers are afraid of goose quills."

Simply put. . . the pen is mightier than the sword.

This belief, and the challenge of this belief, became the underlying motivations for the main characters of our story. The power of the written word has the ability to form ideas and thoughts in people and when it comes to connecting with hearts and minds, words will always win over brute force.

And in our story, those words will last forever.

After two years, we finally had a script that was ready to be presented to the studio. Amy Pascal and Sony Pictures loved what we had done and green-lit it. That was 2005 but then we ran into problems. I always had the idea that this movie should not only be talking heads, but should show the portrait of an amazing city. For that, we wanted to build big sets, shoot on locations and build a twelve-scale model of Elizabethan London—and that turned out to be just too expensive.

A few years went by, and while I was shooting *2012*, I came to a realization. In *2012* we had scenes taking place all over the world, but due to budget restrictions, nearly the entire film was shot on soundstages in Vancouver. How did we accomplish this task? Lots of CGI and blue screen. Inspired by this experience, I asked myself, "Why don't I do this with my Shakespeare project?"

So, instead of bouncing around England trying to utilize expensive locations, we decided we could do the same thing. Shoot background plates in England and then film the actors on a stage, with a minimal number of reusable sets and a lot of CGI. To my amazement and delight, Sony Pictures immediately green-lit the production again, and a few short weeks later, we were on our way to Berlin.

For the first time in more than twenty years, I was going home to make a movie. The thought of going back to where my career began was both comforting and exciting. I was overwhelmed with a sense of nostalgia for my early years as a filmmaker, and I was not expecting the warm reception I received from the German film community as a whole. They opened up their doors for me, and I had access to the very best Germany had to offer.

In this book, you will learn about many of them, some in their own words. But, I have to say, they were some of the most amazing people I have ever had the pleasure to work with.

Like Anna Foerster, a first-time director of photography, who exceeded all expectations. Or Sebastian Krawinkel, production designer extraordinaire, or Lisy Christl, our fabulous costume designer. They all wanted the film to be authentic; they wanted the audience to "feel" and maybe even "smell" the Elizabethan times. In this task they very much succeeded.

And there were so many more. Every one of them, down to the last Extra helped me to bring my vision of the last years of Queen Elizabeth's reign to life. The end result is a film we are all very proud of.

Volker Engel and Marc Weigert, who worked with me on many films before, created the visual effects of *Anonymous*. A difficult assignment, to say the least, because they were tasked to rebuild a realistic, sixteenth-century London in a computer with only limited resources and funds. The work they did is just spectacular!

On the production side was Kirstin Winkler, Larry Franco, and Robert Leger. They and their team had to organize a shoot, which was quite complex and demanding. At the same time, Leo Davis and Lissy Holm, our casting directors, were trying to find what you most need as a director: a terrific cast!

When Rhys Ifans showed up for his meeting at my home in London, dressed like a rock star with wild hair and clothes, I asked him which part he wanted to play. I expected Ben Jonson or William Shakespeare, so you can imagine my surprise when he said, "I have a real affinity to play the Earl of Oxford." I'm sure the look on my face had to be one of shock because my casting director quickly added, "He does 'posh' really well."

And sure enough, his transformation into the character of Edward de Vere was incredible. We had found our "Earl of Oxford."

The same goes for the rest of our wonderful cast. They all out-did themselves, and I am deeply grateful to

"It's quite interesting how emotional people get when it comes to this subject. What we're doing in this movie is very controversial."

9

each of them. The young and extremely talented Sebastian Armesto as Ben Jonson; the great David Thewlis, who had to endure so many hours of make-up to become William Cecil in three different ages; the brilliant Edward Hogg, as his hunchbacked son; master of the stage Sir Derek Jacobi, as the Prologue; and the courageous Rafe Spall, who had the difficult part of playing William Shakespeare. There are naturally many more, and this book will try to sing their praise.

However, if I do have to mention one more actress, or a pair of actresses, whose names were in my head long before casting ever began, it would be Vanessa Redgrave and her daughter, Joely Richardson. Having worked with Joely on *The Patriot*, I was excited to see her grow as an actress over the years, and the likeness between her and her mother was positively amazing. I knew that creating a character that these two amazing actresses could portray at different stages of life would be a challenge made easy

LEFT: *Roland Emmerich on the London Street set.*
ABOVE: *Early concept illustration of sixteenth-century London by Axel Eichhorst.*

by their wealth of talent. They were truly outstanding in this role of Queen Elizabeth.

I have to admit the only thing I was afraid of as a director was to put all these plays onto the stage we built for this film. And what a stage it was. We built a full replica of an Elizabethan theatre *The Rose*, which then, with some redressing, became *The Globe*.

It was such an amazing feeling just to walk onto this set because one instantly understands why the magic of the public theatre was so transforming in the sixteenth century. It was the only public word at the time, delivered to the people without too much censorship. That's where allegory triumphed, symbolically expressing deeper, often moral or political, meanings of things. I was always amazed by how Elizabethan audiences were able to listen and understand what they were seeing, even though most of them lacked the ability to read or write.

I searched for quite some time to find a collaborator to help me bring these plays to life. I knew from the very beginning that I would have to find an accomplished theatre director for this task. But, considering the subject of our film, the person would have to be a very courageous

one. We found our theatre director in Tamara Harvey.

But Tamara would not only have to direct the plays for our film, she would also have to cast all the actors to be in them. I wanted her to form a troupe of players; the same way they existed in Shakespeare's times. And what an amazing troupe she found! I am eternally thankful to these performers and to Tamara for all their wonderful work. I couldn't have done it without them.

Tamara and her players were also responsible for the most magical moment I experienced during shooting. We had just moved into the *Rose* set and we had a house full of extras. Anna had set up her cameras, and everyone was excited to witness the first performance in *our* theatre. The trumpets sounded and the character *Prologue* of *Henry V* steps on stage, played by the incomparable Mark Rylance. What an amazing experience. It was the first words of Shakespeare performed in our film, and we all suddenly forgot that we were on a movie set. We were instantly transformed into the times of Elizabeth I, and for the moment, we all experienced what it must have felt to hear the eternal words of the man we know as William Shakespeare. ❀ *April 2011*

PROLOGUE
The time is out of joint

**INT. BROADWAY THEATRE—BACKSTAGE/
EMPTY STAGE—DUSK**

The curtains are still closed, and the sound of the audience excitedly MURMURING behind them is heard. Stagehands are moving stage lights as—

A STAGE MANAGER

takes a nervous peek through the curtains to check the audience—it's a full house. He holds a prop umbrella in one hand, anxiously checks his watch in the other.

He looks on both wings of the stage—and then relief floods his face as he sees The Man in the Grey Suit hurrying over to him. The Stage Manager wordlessly hands him the umbrella and signals to a stagehand in the background.

The curtains start to OPEN and the MURMUR of the audience dies down.

INT. BROADWAY THEATRE—THE STAGE

The man with the umbrella stands on the empty stage, a single light on him. He is "**PROLOGUE.**"

"Prologue" regards his audience for a beat before:

> PROLOGUE

Soul of the Age!
The applause, delight, the wonder of our stage!
Our Shakespeare, rise . . .
(beat, repeating)
Our William Shakespeare . . . For he is all of ours, is he not? The most performed playwright of all time! The author of 37 plays, 154 sonnets, and several epic poems that are collectively known as the ultimate expressions of humanity in the English language. And yet . . . And yet . . .
(beat)

Not a single manuscript of any kind has ever been found written by Shakespeare. In four hundred years, not one document of any kind— be it poem, play, diary or even a simple letter.
(beat)
He was born the son of a glove-maker, and at some unknown time, armed with but an elementary school education, he went to London where, the story goes, he became an actor and eventually a playwright.

OFF STAGE

A stagehand takes a wooden hammer and beats against a flat metal plate, creating the SOUNDS of THUNDER.

Another stagehand starts to lift shutters in front of a stage light back and forth to create LIGHTNING STRIKES.

ON STAGE

"Prologue" opens his umbrella.

> PROLOGUE *(cont'd)*

He died at the age of 52, and was survived by his wife and two daughters who were, like Shakespeare's own father, irrefutably illiterate.

OFF STAGE

In the rafters a stagehand opens valves. It starts to RAIN.

> PROLOGUE *(O.C.) (cont'd)*

His will famously left his second best bed to his widow. But it made no mention of a single book or manuscript.

The actor who will play "Ben JONSON" (mid 30's) appears in the wings, bearded, ready to go on stage, holding a prop leather manuscript. Behind him a group of Elizabethan "soldiers" strap on their swords.

ON STAGE

"Prologue" continues. . .

PROLOGUE (cont'd)

Is it possible Shakespeare owned no books at his death because . . . he could not read? That he wrote no letters because he, like his father before him and his children after him, could not write?

(lets that sink in, then)

Our Shakespeare is a cypher, a ghost; his biography made not by history . . . but by conjecture. His story not written with facts, but with . . . imagination.

The rain has intensified. "Prologue" turns and the camera starts to leave him . . . .

PROLOGUE (cont'd)

(more energetic)

So! Let me offer you a different story. A darker story . . . Of quills and swords. Of power and betrayal. Of a stage conquered, and a throne lost!

A FLASH OF LIGHTNING, and for a moment only sheets of RAIN are visible. No stage, no "Prologue." Then, through the rain, we see a form of a man . . . Ben Jonson . . . running. Then we make out the shapes of houses . . . a street. *We're not on a stage anymore.* We are:

EXT. BANKSIDE LONDON—1604 NIGHT

Jonson—carrying the manuscript—runs up the street toward a large circular theatre.

He frantically opens the wooden door to the theatre—

INT. THE ROSE THEATRE—NIGHT

—and he quickly bolts it behind him, turns, and desperately looks for a place to hide. . . .

To be, or not to be, that is

ACT 1
THE ARGUMENT

THE LIFE OF
HENRIE THE
FIFTH

DRAMATIS PERSONÆ

KING HENRIE
DUKE of GLOUCESTER
DUKE of BEDFORD
DUKE of EXETER
DUKE of YORK
EARLE of SALISBURY, WEST
MERE and ... WARWICK
ARCHBISHOP of CANTERBURY
BISHOP of ELY
EARL of CAMBRIDGE
LORD of SCROOP
SIR THOMAS GREY
SIR THOMAS ERPINGHAM
GOWER
FLUELLEN   JAMY
MACMORRIS   GOWER
PISTOL   NYM

Prologue

Is
Shakespeare
DEAD?
Mark Twain

For the instruction of the ignorant I will make a list, now, of those details of Shakespeare's history which are *facts*—verified facts, established facts, undisputed facts.

FACTS

- He was born on the 23rd of April, 1564.
- Of good farmer-class parents who could not read, could not write, could not sign their names.
- At Stratford, a small back settlement which in that day was shabby and unclean, and densely illiterate. Of the nineteen important men charged with the government of the town, thirteen had to "make their mark" in attesting important documents, because they could not write their names.
- Of the first eighteen years of his life *nothing* is known. They are a blank.
- On the 27th of November (1582) William Shakespeare took out a license to marry Anne Whateley.
- Next day William Shakespeare took out a license to marry Anne Hathaway. She was eight years his senior.
- William Shakespeare married Anne Hathaway. In a hurry. By grace of a reluctantly-granted dispensation there was but one publication of the banns.
- Within six months the first child was born.
- About two (blank) years followed, during which period *nothing at all happened to Shakespeare*, so far as anybody knows.
- Then came twins—1585. February.
- Two blank years follow.

- Then—1587—he makes a ten-year visit to London, leaving the family behind.
- Five blank years follow. During this period *nothing happened to him*, as far as anybody actually knows.
- Then—1592—there is mention of him as an actor.
- Next year—1593—his name appears in the official list of players.
- Next year—1594—he played before the queen. A detail of no consequence: other obscurities did it every year of the forty-five of her reign. And remained obscure.
- Three pretty full years follow. Full of play-acting. Then in 1597 he bought New Place, Stratford.
- Thirteen or fourteen busy years follow; years in which he accumulated money, and also reputation as actor and manager.
- Meantime his name, liberally and variously spelt, had become associated with a number of great plays and poems, as (ostensibly) author of the same.
- Some of these, in these years and later, were pirated, but he made no protest. Then—1610-11—he returned to Stratford and settled down for good and all, and busied himself in lending money, trading in tithes, trading in land and houses; shirking a debt of forty-one shillings, borrowed by his wife during his long desertion of his family; suing debtors for shillings and coppers; being sued himself for shillings and coppers; and acting as confederate to a neighbor who tried to rob the town of its rights in a certain common, and did not succeed.
- He lived five or six years—till 1616—in the joy of these

> "... a manager, an actor of inferior grade, a small trader in a small village that did not regard him as a person of any consequence, and had forgotten all about him before he was fairly cold in his grave."

elevated pursuits. Then he made a will, and signed each of its three pages with his name.

- A thoroughgoing business man's will. It named in minute detail every item of property he owned in the world—houses, lands, sword, silver-gilt bowl, and so on—all the way down to his "second-best bed" and its furniture.
- It carefully and calculatingly distributed his riches among the members of his family, overlooking no individual of it. Not even his wife: the wife he had been enabled to marry in a hurry by urgent grace of a special dispensation before he was nineteen; the wife whom he had left husbandless so many years; the wife who had had to borrow forty-one shillings in her need, and which the lender was never able to collect of the prosperous husband, but died at last with the money still lacking. No, even this wife was remembered in Shakespeare's will.
- He left her that "second-best bed."
- And *not another thing*; not even a penny to bless her lucky widowhood with.
- It was eminently and conspicuously a business man's will, not a poet's.
- It mentioned *not a single book*.
- Books were much more precious than swords and silver-gilt bowls and second-best beds in those days, and when a departing person owned one he gave it a high place in his will.
- The will mentioned *not a play, not a poem, not an unfinished literary work, not a scrap of manuscript of any kind.*
- Many poets have died poor, but this is the only one in history that has died *this* poor; the others all left literary remains behind. Also a book. Maybe two.
- If Shakespeare had owned a dog—but we need not go into that: we know he would have mentioned it in his will.

If a good dog, Susanna would have got it; if an inferior one his wife would have got a dower interest in it. I wish he had had a dog, just so we could see how painstakingly he would have divided that dog among the family, in his careful business way.

- He signed the will in three places.
- In earlier years he signed two other official documents.
- These five signatures still exist.
- There are *no other specimens of his penmanship in existence*. Not a line.
- Was he prejudiced against the art? His granddaughter, whom he loved, was eight years old when he died, yet she had had no teaching, he left no provision for her education although he was rich, and in her mature womanhood she couldn't write and couldn't tell her husband's manuscript from anybody else's—she thought it was Shakespeare's.
- When Shakespeare died in Stratford *it was not an event*. It made no more stir in England than the death of any other forgotten theatre-actor would have made. Nobody came down from London; there were no lamenting poems, no eulogies, no national tears—there was merely silence, and nothing more. A striking contrast with what happened when Ben Jonson, and Francis Bacon, and Spenser, and Raleigh and the other distinguished literary folk of Shakespeare's time passed from life! No praiseful voice was lifted for the lost Bard of Avon; even Ben Jonson waited seven years before he lifted his.
- *So far as anybody actually knows and can prove*, Shakespeare of Stratford-on-Avon never wrote a play in his life.
- *So far as anybody knows and can prove*, he never wrote a letter to anybody in his life.
- *So far as any one knows, he received only one letter during his life.*

So far as any one *knows and can prove*, Shakespeare of Stratford wrote only one poem during his life. This one is authentic. He did write that one—a fact which stands undisputed; he wrote the whole of it; he wrote the whole of it out of his own head. He commanded that this work of art be engraved upon his tomb, and he was obeyed. There it abides to this day. This is it:

> Good friend for Iesus sake forbeare
> To digg the dust encloased heare:
> Blest be ye man yt spares thes stones
> And curst be he yt moves my bones.

In the list as above set down, will be found *every positively known* fact of Shakespeare's life, lean and meagre as the invoice is. Beyond these details we know *not a thing* about him. All the rest of his vast history, as furnished by the biographers, is built up, course upon course, of guesses, inferences, theories, conjectures—an Eiffel Tower of artificialities rising sky-high from a very flat and very thin foundation of inconsequential facts.

Isn't it odd, when you think of it: that you may list all the celebrated Englishmen, Irishmen, and Scotchmen of modern times, clear back to the first Tudors—a list containing five hundred names, shall we say?—and you can go to the histories, biographies and cyclopedias and learn the particulars of the lives of every one of them. Every one of them except one—the most famous, the most renowned—by far the most illustrious of them all—Shakespeare! You can get the details of the lives of all the celebrated ecclesiastics in the list; all the celebrated tragedians, comedians, singers, dancers, orators, judges, lawyers, poets, dramatists, historians, biographers, editors, inventors, reformers, statesmen, generals, admirals, discoverers, prize-fighters, murderers, pirates, conspirators, horse-jockeys, bunco-steerers, misers, swindlers, explorers, adventurers by land and sea, bankers, financiers, astronomers, naturalists, Claimants, impostors, chemists, biologists, geologists, philologists, college presidents and professors, architects, engineers, painters, sculptors, politicians, agitators, rebels, revolutionists, patriots, demagogues, clowns, cooks, freaks, philosophers, burglars, highwaymen, journalists, physicians, surgeons—you can get the life-histories of all of them but *one*. Just one—the most extraordinary and the most celebrated of them all—Shakespeare!

You may add to the list the thousand celebrated persons furnished by the rest of Christendom in the past four centuries, and you can find out the life-histories of all those people, too. You will then have listed 1500 celebrities, and you can trace the authentic life-histories of the whole of them. Save one—far and away the most colossal prodigy of the entire accumulation—Shakespeare! About him you can find out *nothing*. Nothing of even the slightest importance. Nothing worth the trouble of stowing away in your memory. Nothing that even remotely indicates that he was ever anything more than a distinctly common-place person—a manager, an actor of inferior grade, a small trader in a small village that did not regard him as a person of any consequence, and had forgotten all about him before he was fairly cold in his grave. We can go to the records and find out the life-history of every renowned *race-horse* of modern times—but not Shakespeare's! There are many reasons why, and they have been furnished in cartloads (of guess and conjecture) by those troglodytes; but there is one that is worth all the rest of the reasons put together, and is abundantly sufficient all by itself—*he hadn't any history to record*. There is no way of getting around that deadly fact. And no sane way has yet been discovered of getting around its formidable significance.

Its quite plain significance—to any but those thugs (I do not use the term unkindly) is, that Shakespeare had no prominence while he lived, and none until he had been dead two or three generations. The Plays enjoyed high fame from the beginning; and if he wrote them it seems a pity the world did not find it out. He ought to have explained that he was the author, and not merely a *nom de plume* for another man to hide behind. If he had been less intemperately solicitous about his bones, and more solicitous about his Works, it would have been better for his good name, and a kindness to us. The bones were not important. They will moulder away, they will turn to dust, but the Works will endure until the last sun goes down. ❀

~

Mark Twain is the pen name of Samuel Clemens, an American humorist, satirist, lecturer, writer, and riverboat pilot. He is best known for the classic American novels The Adventures of Tom Sawyer *and* Adventures of Huckleberry Finn. Is Shakespeare Dead? *was first published in April 1909.*

Edward Vere 17th Earle of Oxfo[rd]
Lord high Chamberlaine of Eng[land]
Married 1st Ann Daughter [to]
Wm Cecil Lord Burghley 2nd
Eliz Daughter to Thos Trent[ham]
of Roucester in Com: Sta[ff]
and died 24th of June 16[04]

Shakespeare's
LOST KINGDOM

Charles Beauclerk

Why should Shakespeare's identity be a matter for doubt? He lived in a well-documented age—the age of Elizabeth—and his plays enthralled both the theatre-going public and the two monarchs who reigned over him. The notion that he was somehow anonymous in the London of his time is surely untenable, or at least as perverse as claiming that Mozart was invisible in the Vienna of the 1780s when his immortal operas were being written and produced. Shakespeare—surely?—must have been one of the most celebrated and lionized figures of his day. After all, Ben Jonson hailed him as a poet to whom all Europe "homage owe[d]."

Yet anonymous is exactly what he was. Despite the lowly background claimed for him, he never appears to have sought the patronage of a nobleman or courtier for his dramas, and his first published works appeared without a name on the title-page. Concerning his character and activities his contemporaries were mute; even his plays provoked little overt comment. When he died, no one thought his passing worthy of notice. But then much of his life, if we are to believe the professors, was spent in rustic obscurity, trading wool and prosecuting fellow townsmen for small sums—a perspective enshrined in the original monument erected in the Stratford church in the early 1620s, which depicts a mean-faced merchant hugging a sack of wool. Shakespeare's public greatness can only be

OPPOSITE: *Edward de Vere, 17th Earl of Oxford, artist unknown.*

said to have begun posthumously in 1623, seven years after his death, when the First Folio of his collected plays was published with a stirring eulogy by fellow dramatist Ben Jonson, saluting his rival as the "soul of the age."

So, how could the soul of the age be Mr. Nobody? Simply opening the First Folio and glancing through the plays provides a strong clue. These are court dramas written by a court insider who had suffered a fall from grace, and was using the theatre to tell his story in much the same way that Hamlet does. And what a tale he had to tell! Murder and incest in the highest places. No wonder he was silenced, Soviet-style, his name swept from the records.

Rather than arguing for a widespread conspiracy in Elizabethan London, I propose that the mysterious silence surrounding Shakespeare's life and identity reflects the social mores of an insular and self-serving court, of which the playwright was a prominent member. Courtiers knew that here was an author who did not scruple to treat of state affairs, hence it was in their interest to protect his true identity—that way they shielded their venal world from the scrutiny of outsiders. Exposing the author would have meant exposing his satires of them and their Queen. To those at court, then, Shakespeare's identity was an open secret, rather like President Kennedy's philandering, which, while it was common knowledge amongst White House staff, never leaked into the press.

Tracing Shakespeare's origins means following the secret early love life of England's most celebrated queen. When King Henry VIII died in 1547 his daughter, Prin-

In January 1549, the very month that Seymour was executed for plotting to marry Elizabeth and abduct the eleven-year-old king, Elizabeth wrote to the Lord Protector to defend herself against what she described as "these shameful slanders." It is probable, however, that she had already given birth by the time she wrote the letter, and that her trusted adviser William Cecil (the future Lord Burghley) arranged for the boy to be adopted by the de Vere family, Earls of Oxford. The bastard child was named Edward, no doubt in honor of Elizabeth's younger brother, Edward VI, for the name sticks out like a sore thumb in the long line of Aubreys and Johns that preceded the boy in the Earldom of Oxford. And if this changeling (the future 17th Earl of Oxford) grew up to be "Shake-speare," the son of the "virgin queen," then his obsession with the royal succession is no longer an aberration, but the natural outgrowth of his dispossession. His plays, after all, are filled with disinherited princes or kings-who-are-not-kings (Hamlet, Lear, Richard II, Henry VI, Prince Hal, Falconbridge, the Duke of York, Prospero, even Bottom), so much so that one could accuse Shakespeare of suffering from a "king-complex."

From infancy Oxford's life was planned out and managed by Sir William Cecil, Elizabeth's chief minister and troubleshooter for four decades, and the most powerful man in the kingdom. When Edward de Vere's foster father, the 16th Earl of Oxford, died in 1562, the thirteen-year-old Edward was sent to live at Cecil House on the Strand under the eagle eye of its patriarch, now his guardian-in-law. Despite the twenty-four-hour surveillance, there were compensations, for Burghley had one of the finest libraries in the land and imported the latest works of history and philosophy from the Continent. He also had the best minds at his beck and call to tutor the budding genius and make of him a true Renaissance prince. Both politically and culturally it placed the young Oxford at the cutting edge. Burghley was the consummate politician, Oxford the supreme poet: they saw the world from opposite perspectives. It was an uneasy relationship at the best of times and one made more fraught when Oxford was married to Burghley's pliant daughter, Anne Cecil (as part of the older man's covert plan to control the throne and transfuse royal blood into Cecil veins).

Oxford grew up a divided personality, never quite

cess Elizabeth, was sent to live with the king's widow, Katherine Parr, at Chelsea. Within months Katherine had remarried her old love, Lord Admiral Thomas Seymour, a vauntingly ambitious man who took a wanton (and political) interest in the fourteen-year-old princess. Seymour wooed Elizabeth with ever increasing boldness, and the two were caught *in flagrante* by his distressed wife. Soon it was bruited at court that Elizabeth was pregnant with Seymour's child. As a result, in May 1548, Elizabeth was sent away to Cheshunt in Hertfordshire far from the roving eye of her stepfather. There she "fell sick," taking to her bed for the better part of three months. In London, however, the word was that she was in childbed. Years later, in her memoirs, Jane Dormer, Duchess of Feria, referred to reports that a baby had been born of the illicit union and "miserably destroyed." But given the Tudor failure to produce healthy male issue, it is unlikely that a boy child would have been dispatched when a home could be found with a trusted noble family.

certain which face to turn to the world. Scholarly and deeply sensitive, he was also a gifted sportsman with a flair for horsemanship and the joust. Pride and touchiness were never far from the surface, and he was painfully conscious of the royalty that circumstances had forced him to suppress. Bastardy shamed him, and one of the first poems he wrote bewailed the loss of his good name. In 1569, when he came of age, he took matters in his own hands and began to sign his name using what has come to be called the "crown signature." His name was surmounted by a crown, while underneath, running the full length of the signature, was a line with seven dashes through it, as if to signify King Edward VII. Indeed the whole signature is shaped like a crown. It was a bold assertion of identity, and a message to Burghley and the Queen that he expected to be acknowledged for who he was.

Oxford was on a collision course with Elizabeth. He wanted truth to prevail over policy, while the Queen, a mistress of prevarication, preferred to keep things in a state of suspension and postponement. She knew that to acknowledge her son was to let the skeletons out of the royal cupboard. To complicate matters, she and Oxford (her son) were powerfully attracted to one another, with Elizabeth using sex to control him: first, to keep his hopes of succession simmering, and then to divert them towards another, more suitable heir. This other was the fruit of their trespass, "the fairest bud that red rose [Elizabeth] ever bare," a royal heir twice over, who like Oxford before him was placed with a noble foster family. Born in the summer of 1574, he grew up as Henry Wriothesley, 3rd Earl of Southampton, and it was to him that Oxford/Shakespeare dedicated *Venus and Adonis* twenty years later. The story of his birth and the battles over his custody are told more fully in *A Midsummer Night's Dream*, where he is described as the "little western flower."

So many letters of the time have been judiciously lost that it is hard at this remove to gauge the sort of scandal that Oxford's incestuous affair with Elizabeth caused at court and the ostracism he suffered as a result. But despite the shadow of his "wrong," Oxford was the brightest star

OPPOSITE: *William Cecil, 1st Baron Burghley, unknown artist, after 1572.* ABOVE: *Queen Elizabeth I, unknown artist, late 17th century.*

in the Queen's firmament: a poet-playwright who wrote courtly entertainments, danced, jousted, and excelled all others in the cut and thrust of witty repartee. He was well travelled too, especially in Italy, where he had a house built in Venice and took part in the Commedia dell'arte. When he returned home he brought with him a new vision of art that sparked the English Renaissance. Indeed, so profound was the influence of Italy on Oxford, both artistically and sartorially, that he was soon being satirized as the Italianate Englishman. King or no king, he lived like one, leaving a trail of tailors' bills across London.

Sooner or later it was inevitable that Elizabeth would betray Oxford to his Puritan opponents; it was easier to sacrifice her son than her carefully crafted reputation. In retaliation Oxford set up his own renegade court at Fisher's Folly in Bishopsgate. It was here in the 1580s that the golden age of Elizabethan literature was born with dazzling productions at court and the Blackfriars. Oxford had two acting companies under his patronage, Oxford's

"He employed an intermediary or frontman—a not uncommon practice in Elizabethan times—and many have speculated that William Shakspere, the man from Stratford, played this shady role for a share of Oxford's hush money."

Men and Oxford's Boys, and created a stir by appearing on stage himself. Elizabeth soon realized that she needed to secure Oxford's anonymity, otherwise the plays would be seen for the sedition that they were: hence the £1,000 annuity she granted Oxford in 1586, a sugar-coated pill if ever there was one, but far too tempting for the down-at-heels Earl. No wonder he has Hamlet cry, "I'll take the ghost's word for a thousand pound," i.e, he will be a ghost-writer for his £1,000 a year. The Queen's money was well spent, for later, in the 1590s, Oxford refashioned many of his works and, breaking the class taboo, took them to the public theatres. For this he employed an intermediary or frontman—a not uncommon practice in Elizabethan times—and many have speculated that William Shakspere, the man from Stratford, played this shady role for a share of Oxford's hush money.

The first time the name William Shakespeare appeared in print, it was affixed to the dedication of *Venus and Adonis*, a 1200-line poem that told the story of the Goddess of Love's baleful passion for a beautiful youth. When it was published in 1593, it would have been recognized as an allegory of Queen Elizabeth's sexual pursuit of the poet "Shake-speare." In essence, it describes how Adonis (Shakespeare/Oxford) rejects the love of the goddess (Elizabeth), because he knows she is his mother. Stung by his rejection, the goddess kills the dazzling boy in the form of a boar, and from his blood springs up a purple flower. The murder is not literal, but describes the young man's death as the son of the goddess and his rebirth as an artist, symbolized by the flower. It is also a metaphor for sexual union, with the boar's tusk piercing Adonis, and the purple flower representing the couple's royal child. An instant bestseller, the book-length poem appeared around the time of the Queen's sixtieth birthday when the question of the royal succession was coming to a head. At all events, the creation of the most celebrated name in literature, which the poet refers to as his "invention," is forever associated with a poem advertising the dynastic secrets of the House of Tudor.

In sum, Oxford's story is that of a brilliant court maverick whose early stardom was blighted by a dramatic fall from grace and the growing mistrust of his peers. The fall camouflaged a deep crisis of identity, compounded by a sin that dared not speak its name, and in no time a Renaissance prince had been transformed into a nobody. The theatre was his means of recovering his status and identity at a deeper level, as well as a way of defying the "chronicles" and recording his truth for posterity. It was through the theatre, too, that he reminded the Queen of her responsibility towards the truth they shared, both personally and nationally.

The purpose of the Oxfordian approach is to reconnect Shakespeare with his works, as well as his motives, a task that enables us to discover why he wrote what he wrote. It is also a way of restoring his humanity, and the story of Shakespeare's humanity is infinitely more interesting than the story of his genius. If he gave us a richer and more conscious humanity, then it is time to reciprocate that gift by making him fully human again. We can do this by acting on Hamlet's appeal to Horatio to tell his story to "the yet unknowing world." ❀

~

Charles Beauclerk writes on sixteenth- and seventeenth-century history, and is a former president of the Shakespeare Oxford Society. His most recent book Shakespeare's Lost Kingdom *was published by Grove Press in 2010.*

Opposite: *The Cobbe Portrait of William Shakespeare, unknown artist, ca. 1610.*

They have their exits and their entrances

ACT II
THE PLAYERS
and one man in his time plays many parts.

Earl of Oxford
EDWARD DE VERE *(1550–1604)*
Rhys Ifans

Edward de Vere, the 17th Earl of Oxford, was born at Hedingham Castle into a very important and well-connected English family. He was a soldier, scholar, venture capitalist, world traveler, playwright, poet, patron of the arts—supporting authors, musicians and actors—and a champion jouster. In short he was a true renaissance man.

When he was twelve his father died and he became a ward of Queen Elizabeth who placed him in the care of her trusted advisor, William Cecil. When he turned twenty-one he took his place in the House of Lords and married Cecil's daughter Anne—a poet in her own right who is thought by some to be the inspiration for Ophelia in *Hamlet*. The Queen attended the wedding. And though Edward was wildly popular at court his favor with the queen waxed and waned and after an affair with her majesty's Lady of the Bedchamber, Anne Vavasour, he was banished for a time.

As if touring the continent, fighting the Spanish Armada, being attacked by pirates, writing plays and poetry, maintaining a band of tumblers and two acting troupes (Oxford's Men and Oxford's Boys), and entering jousting contests didn't keep him busy enough, he also petitioned the queen to gain rights to import oils, fruit and wool, to farm the tin mines of Cornwall, to be the Governor of the Isle of Jersey, and to be the President of Wales. He was granted none of those.

He died in June 1604 of unknown causes and was remembered by his contemporaries as being an outstanding poet at court and as a leading patron of the arts.

Three hundred and sixteen years later, in 1920, an English school teacher named J. Thomas Looney wrote a book called *Shakespeare Identified* arguing "that there was no sufficient evidence that the man William Shakspere had written the works with which he was credited," concluding that "the ultimate verdict will be to proclaim Edward de Vere, Seventeenth Earl of Oxford, as the real author."

In *Anonymous* the Earl of Oxford is played by the very talented Rhys Ifans, who though not totally convinced of the Oxfordian theory, admits it is a story that has intrigued and excited him. "I've always really loved Shakespeare—being moved both by performing and watching it—and I felt in school, and

certainly now, that he is somehow hidden from us. Shakespeare's just like this voice in a void in a vacuum, and we don't really know the guy who wrote the works."

Ifans' passion for the authorship topic grew during production as he totally immersed himself in the role. Director Roland Emmerich says, "He did an incredible job in the film. He would come to work as Rhys Ifans, but as soon as he came out of hair and make-up and put his costume on, he behaved differently—he transformed into Edward de Vere."

Ifans, found the character of Oxford fascinating. "I told Roland that if he wanted an easy ride, he could offer me Shakespeare, but if he wanted to be brave, he should give me a crack at Oxford, and he did! He seemed to like

my reading, but I guess he had to convince certain powers that be that I was capable of sustaining the Queen's English for long periods of time and of behaving like a true aristocrat." Emmerich and Ifans had quite a few discussions about Oxford in terms of his visual appearance, social position and his mysterious aloofness, coupled with danger and a flightiness. Ifans says, "Between the two of us, we came up with the bastard son of David Bowie and Karl Lagerfeld!"

Born and raised in Wales, Rhys Ifans is one of Britain's finest contemporary actors. He attended youth acting schools at Theatre Clwyd, Mold and appeared in many Welsh language television programs before embarking on his film career. His breakout performance came in 1999

in *Notting Hill*, opposite Julia Roberts and Hugh Grant. Younger fans know him from *Nanny McPhee and the Big Bang*, and as Luna Lovegood's father in *Harry Potter and the Deathly Hallows*.

Now, in *Anonymous*, he gets to play Oxford as the true author of Shakespeare's work. "The character is different to things people may have seen me in before. Oxford is his own man and his own creation. His mind is a huge, swirling mass of richness, bursting at the seams—which is Shakespeare's mind." ✿

Young
OXFORD
Jamie Campbell Bower

Screenwriter John Orloff provides insight about young Oxford, "Young Edward de Vere was raised in William Cecil's household. And Cecil was a pretty strict religious man who didn't believe in poetry and drama as art—he thought it was the work of the devil—and was broadly against them. But when Oxford was a young man, a teenager, he actually published what we would call Shakespearean Sonnets under his own name, Edward de Vere."

Explaining why Oxford would have later concealed his identity, Orloff continues, "You need to put yourself in sixteenth-century Elizabethan England which is a very different culture and society than we live in today. It was not celebrity focused, and in fact, being a playwright or poet, while fine for commoners wasn't fine for noblemen. You could publish a little book of poetry when you were a teenager, but later on it would have been published anonymously. And that happened quite a bit."

English actor Jamie Campbell Bower, while best known as the magically skilled Gellert Grindelwald in *Harry Potter and the Deathly Hallows* and Caius the vampire in *New Moon* and *Breaking Dawn*, is happy to take on the more down-to-earth role of nobleman and poet Edward de Vere. ✿

Older Queen
(1533 – 1603) ELIZABETH
Vanessa Redgrave

Born a princess, demoted to bastard (and Lady) before her third birthday, reinstated as princess, and eventually queen, Elizabeth remains one of Britain's most popular rulers. Also know as The Virgin Queen, Gloriana, and Good Queen Bess, she presided over a golden age in England, a time when the arts flourished and England became one of the most powerful, prosperous countries in the world.

Elizabeth, daughter of Henry VIII, was the survivor of a highly dysfunctional family. Her mother Anne Boleyn (accused of incest, adultery, and witchcraft) was beheaded on her father's orders and four stepmothers followed in eight years—none of whom worked out well. Even Catherine Parr (wife number six), who did her best to hold the damaged Tudors together, went wrong by marrying overly-ambitious Thomas Seymour shortly after the death of Henry VIII. Seymour, uncle to Elizabeth's brother King Edward VI, not only paid inappropriate attention to the thirteen-year-old princess, but he inadvertently put her under suspicion of plotting against the king, an extremely serious offense. Seymour was beheaded, and again, Elizabeth survived. When her older sister Mary—daughter of Catherine of Aragon and an ardent Catholic—took the throne, she briefly locked Elizabeth up in the Tower in fear of her Protestant leanings. It was a tumultuous time.

Still, as a child she had the best tutors and was quite bright. She excelled at her studies—speaking five languages—and took a keen interest in both sports and the arts. She went hawking, hunted stag and deer with her courtiers, rode horse well into her sixties, and was an enthusiastic spectator at tennis matches, jousting, and even bear baiting. She played the lute and the virginals (a sort of harpsichord), loved plays (keeping her own company of actors called the Queen's Players), and adored any kind of pageantry and dancing.

Though she never married, she had many suitors—the most eligible dukes, princes, and kings of Europe—and while she was cleverly able to use her singleness as a political tool at first, it turned into a bit of a drawback as eventually it became apparent she would never produce an heir. The succession of the throne was always a major issue. The closest she came to marrying was to Robert Dudley, Earl of Leicester. They'd known each other since childhood and had been jailed together in the Tower of London, but he

"I would say that the time of Elizabeth I is full of more contradictions, more developments, more intricate politics than any time proceeding it; indeed, our times are somewhat horrifyingly similar!"

was the son of a traitor and his wife was found dead under mysterious circumstances—he was highly unpopular.

Elizabeth was known for choosing good council, chief among them William Cecil, Lord Burghley, who worked behind the scenes to help secure a smooth succession. Though he died in 1598 his son, Robert Cecil, took his place at court and when the time came was able to peacefully place James VI of Scotland (James I of England) on the throne.

Vanessa Redgrave has played a multitude of roles in her film career, from Leonie in *Morgan: A Suitable Case for Treatment*, for which she won the Cannes Film Festival Best Actress Award in 1966, to her leading role as Volumnia in Ralph Fiennes's film of Shakespeare's play *Coriolanus*, which opens in the United States in December 2011. "I've wanted to play Queen Elizabeth I since I read Lytton Strachey's biography *Elizabeth and Essex*," she says. "So I was delighted when Roland Emmerich asked me to play the old queen, and my daughter Joely to play young Elizabeth."

Rhys Ifans, who plays Oxford, sees Redgrave as born to play the part. "She is a formidable, professional, generous, inquisitive, hungry artist. I love her. She's just utterly spellbinding to be on set with," he says. But it's not the first time he's worked with her, "My first paid employment in the theatre was as a trainee flyman for Vanessa's *Taming of the Shrew*. So I spent the first four months of my career watching the top of Vanessa's head from about seventy feet up. It was great to meet her face to face finally."

Anonymous portrays Oxford and Queen Elizabeth as lovers, and its version of the "Virgin Queen" is not exactly what the mainstream audience has been taught. Historically, she was known as a great ruler with her head ruling her heart, but in this story, we see a different side to Elizabeth. She is volatile, passionate and really struggles to find her feet. She's a very full-blooded woman and not this virgin queen that people might have imagined.

Redgrave sums up the era. "I would say that the time of Elizabeth I is full of more contradictions, more developments, more intricate politics than any time proceeding it; indeed, our times are somewhat horrifyingly similar!"

About the Oxfordian theory she says, "I am sure at this point in my life that the actor William Shakespeare could not have conceivably written all those superb plays and poems. It seems more than possible that the author was in fact the Earl of Oxford. I remember how Senator McCarthy's House of Un-American Activities Committee in the 1950s created a situation where a number of excellent writers could not be employed. Other writers agreed to put their names officially to film scripts, were officially paid for these, and then gave the fee to the true 'begetters' of the scripts. There are many question marks over the authorship of Shakespeare's plays, and I love people like our director Roland Emmerich who ask questions and explore possible answers. *Anonymous* is an enthralling story, and I think that finally this is what counts the most." ✿

Young Queen
ELIZABETH
Joely Richardson

Joely Richardson has played her fair share of royalty: from Marie Antoinette in the 2001 film *The Affair of the Necklace* to two fictional princesses—in the 1991 comedy *King Ralph* and in Jim Henson's *The Storyteller*; she also played the woman who was never granted the title of Queen and arguably caused the biggest stir the British monarchy has ever known as Wallis Simpson in *Wallis & Edward*, and, most recently, had the role of Catherine Parr (stepmother to her character in *Anonymous*) in the TV drama *The Tudors*. It is also interesting to note that Joely has three times been offered (and declined) to play the iconic Princess Diana. But the role of Elizabeth I was one she ultimately could not resist.

And it turns out playing a younger version of the same role in the same film as her mother is not new to her either. She began her career portraying—via flashbacks—the younger version of the leading character played by her mother, Vanessa Redgrave, in the 1985 film *Weatherby*.

"At first there were no flashbacks in the script," says director Roland Emmerich. "I was working with John Orloff on an early version of the screenplay when he asked me how I planned to do all these different time spots. When I suggested flashbacks—because it's important to understand where Edward de Vere comes from—he said, 'Well then we'll have to have two casts.' That's when I first came up with the Vanessa Redgrave/Joely Richardson idea."

Richardson adds, "As an actress, it doesn't get much better than playing Elizabeth, but Mum and I both playing the role was an added attraction. For a little while, it didn't look like the dates for us both would work out and while selfishly I wanted the part, I felt that Mum must absolutely play this character. Thankfully it all worked out and the night the offer came through we happened to be together and we were ecstatic that we both got to play this

role in this particular film. We didn't work on gestures or vocal intonations because we assumed that the similarities would already be there and anything contrived would just stand out a mile."

Contemplating the younger/older division of the role, Redgrave says, "A young woman who became queen under dangerous circumstances and who was continually in great personal jeopardy would be a very different person from the sixty-year-old. And one of the storylines in the film concerns who that different person is." With a wry smile she adds, "In the end neither Joely nor I are playing the part in our own way. We are playing Elizabeth in Roland's way."

Joely Richardson and Roland Emmerich last worked together in 2000 on the film *The Patriot*. Richardson says, "As an actor, there is something really nice about working with someone a second or third time because that very rarely happens in our work. And it's so exciting to be part of a project that Roland has such a grand passion for. *Anonymous* is very much breaking his usual roots of action, but it's especially exciting to see him do that; his recreation of sixteenth-century England alone is breathtaking . . . and something we have never seen before!" ✿

41

Lord Burghley
WILLIAM CECIL *(1521 – 1598)*
David Thewlis

The founder of the Cecil family fortune seems to have been William's grandfather, David, who came to England from Wales and turned up as Henry VII's Yeoman of the Guard (a bodyguard). He was promoted to Sergeant-of-Arms under Henry VIII and eventually became Sheriff of Northampton-shire, the country's head law enforcement officer.

William's father, Richard Cecil, worked his way from royal page, through Groom of the Robes (attendant to the king), to Sheriff of Rutland. Even better, he was granted a great deal of land (confiscated from monasteries as England went from Catholic to Protestant) under Henry VIII. And by the third generation the Cecils managed to move from small gentry to British Nobility when Queen Elizabeth elevated William to Baron Burghley upon the marriage of his daughter Anne to Edward de Vere, the Earl of Oxford.

William was well educated, studying at Cambridge and Gray's Inn (a law school). His first wife died young and his second wife, Mildred, was one of the most educated women in the country. He was a faithful husband and devoted father. He loved books and his hobbies were genealogy and heraldry.

Early in his career he worked for Edward Seymour, Lord Protector of young King Edward VI. This association, unfortunately, landed him in the Tower for a time when Seymour was yanked from power and those around him fell too. He survived and eventually became one of the king's Secretaries of State.

In 1561 he was appointed Master of the Court of Wards, a position established under Henry VIII whose job was to administer revenue collected under a kind of feudal tax system, and in conjunction with that, he was responsible for the upbringing and administration of the estates of orphaned nobility. He personally raised Edward de Vere, Earl of Oxford, Henry Wriothesley, Earl of Southampton and Roger Manners, Earl of Rutland (who some theorize is the "true" Shakespeare).

When Elizabeth came to power she chose Cecil immediately as her main advisor. During her reign he served different official roles at different times including Secretary of State, Lord High Treasurer, and Lord Privy Seal. Not known as a great or original thinker, he was a cautious man who was good at avoiding danger. The Marquess of Winchester was quoted as saying, "He was sprung from the willow rather than the oak," meaning he could bend with the ever-changing political winds. He wasn't a religious purist, but believed order was the best way forward and that the sovereign—the ultimate law—was the way to go. Thus, while he was certainly Protestant-leaning, under Mary the country (and he) were Catholic, but under Elizabeth he was Protestant.

Above all he had a strong work ethic and a sense of duty to Elizabeth and, even more perhaps, to the country. He was by far her most important minister—even taking on jobs she had no taste for, such as dealing with her cousin Mary Queen of Scots, and in the end, secretly arranging the succession of the throne, an issue Elizabeth avoided like the plague.

Director Roland Emmerich was thrilled to have award-winning David Thewlis play Queen Elizabeth's chief advisor, William Cecil. "Cecil is such a wonderful villain," says Thewlis, "such a loathsome, perfidious, manipulative character, and I always prefer those kind of roles. He's based on a true character, so I was able to do lots of research, but for the purpose of this story, he's controlling the puppet strings with a motivation—which may or may not be true—of trying to fix the succession of the throne for his own personal ambitions. He's been portrayed in the past as a very kindly old fellow, but considering his position and the politics of the era—the Elizabethan age is filled with true horror—I can't believe he was an avuncular soul."

Thewlis continues, "It's a very substantial role to understand and to play, not least because he ages so much. Elizabeth is played by Joely Richardson and Vanessa Redgrave, but I'm all the way through, and it's a challenge not to caricature it. I don't want to do stooped-old-man-with-a-croaky-voice acting because my dad's eighty-two and he's not stooped and doddery. But then I considered this is an eighty-two-year-old man in Elizabethan England where people didn't live much beyond thirty or forty. In this case the make-up—though it took four and a half hours when he's at his oldest, and was quite tedious—is definitely helpful since it's done so well. It makes you feel differently, move differently." He adds with a laugh, "And it makes you feel very good at the end of the day when you take it off because you look so young."

David also had a special tutor in preparation for his role. "I live in Windsor, quite close to the castle so the history is right there on my doorstep. My neighbor, Sir Peter, is a knight of the garter and has given me personal tours of the castle. He's a wonderful history teacher. It's been really special to be there thinking Cecil was right here," says Thewlis.

David Thewlis is hoping that the film will make Shakespeare's works—no matter who wrote them—more accessible to a wider audience, "It's a very theatrical film. You actually get to see a lot of stage pieces being performed as they would have been seen in Shakespeare's time, and there is so much beauty, so much passion, so much pain and so much horror in his plays. We owe a lot to him; the proliferation of language and poetry goes right back to Shakespeare, and I think that's worth anyone knowing about." ❀

Earl of Salisbury
(1563 – 1612) **ROBERT CECIL**
Edward Hogg

Robert Cecil went into the family business of loyal service to the crown. Beside taking over as chief minister to Queen Elizabeth upon his father William's death, he also served as Secretary of State, Chancellor of the Duchy of Lancaster, Lord Privy Seal, and Lord High Treasurer. Sir Robert Naunton wrote at the time, "He was his father's own son, he was a courtier from his cradle, and had . . . the tutorship of the times and Court, which were then the academies of art and cunning."

Historian John Brewer said, "He was sickly from his youth; and with the exception of a handsome but pale face, and dark, melancholy eyes, he was not qualified by the graces of his person to shine in the gay throng that crowded round the Queen, or take part in the amusements of a Court, where every lady was expected to dance, and every gentleman to wear a sword and seek occasions for using it. A head, squarely set on rounded and disproportioned shoulders, gave him the appearance of being deformed; and the effect was exaggerated by the dress and fashion of the times." He was only five feet two inches tall.

Though it was said he had no friends at court and many detractors, the queen took a liking to him—or at least a protective stance—and he was one of the few in Elizabeth's service to survive completely unscathed.

Robert wrote to his father William in a letter, "I received a gracious message from her Majesty, under her sporting name of 'pigmy,' bidding me to take care of my health, and looking to hear from me." Sometimes she called him "little man," or "elf." From Elizabeth, anyway, he seemed to take it in good humor.

Perhaps his most important achievement was orchestrating the successful transition of the throne from the childless Queen Elizabeth to the Scottish King James, something he worked on in secret.

Within three hours of the queen's death, Cecil led the Council in drawing up a proclamation naming James king.

As a show of appreciation James stopped at the Cecil estate, Theobalds, on his way to London and raised his host to nobility with the title Baron Cecil of Essendon. Later he was created Viscount Cranborne, Earl of Salisbury, and in 1606 he was knighted.

"In the story we're telling, Robert Cecil—along with his father William—is seen as the villain. And what attracted me to the role was that the script made him seem more human, no worse than any of the other characters," says rising star Edward Hogg, who plays Robert Cecil. "They are all power hungry, waging their own power struggles. I like the fact that in our story you are able to see the reasons behind his choices." He continues, "But it's fun to play bad guys anyway."

Hair and make-up in the film certainly help transform him. "It completely changes who I am and what I look like," he says, "plus I have a limp—and a hump. The make-up is so extraordinary, in fact, that one day I was on set without make-up when John Orloff, the writer, came up to me and said, 'Have you seen that Hogg? I need to give him his rewrites.' And I said, 'Are you kidding me? It's me.' It's happened a few times. I don't know whether that means I'm really horrendous as Robert Cecil or as me."

He concludes saying, "Anyway I feel like the luckiest guy in the world. I get to play that little bit more extreme character, so I get to have a bit more fun. It's been my favorite job ever." ❀

Earl of Southampton
(1573 – 1624) HENRY WRIOTHESLEY
Xavier Samuel

Henry Wriothesley—pronounced *Risley*—the 3rd Earl of Southampton is best remembered as a courtier and literary patron, most notably as Shakespeare's. And though Southampton was an enthusiastic fan of the arts he was also broke until about 1597 and so had more good cheer than cash to offer in those days.

Still Shakespeare's poems *Venus and Adonis* and *The Rape of Lucrece* were dedicated to him, and some suspect that Southampton was the "Fair Youth"—described as "lascivious" and "sensual"—of Shakespeare's sonnets. By all accounts Southampton did have an almost feminine beauty with long flowing auburn hair, but by 1594 Shakespeare had found a paying job with the Lord Chamberlain's Men acting troupe while Southampton was attending to his other interests: going on military expeditions and making friends at court (becoming friendly with arch rivals Essex and Robert Cecil both).

Unfortunately, in the end he sided with Essex in support of his rebellion and was convicted of treason and condemned to death. Fortunately, his friend Cecil argued successfully that "the poor Earl of Southampton," merely for the love of Essex, "had been drawn into this action," and had his sentence reduced to life in prison.

When James I took the throne, Southampton was released from jail, regained his title, was knighted and given the wine monopoly that Elizabeth had taken from Essex (which partially caused the rebellion in the first place). Later in life he spent his time, and considerable fortune, as a sort of armchair pioneer equipping an expedition to Virginia, joining the East India Company and helping Henry Hudson on his way in search of the Northwest Passage.

Southampton died, along with his eldest son, in the Netherlands while leading a troop of English volunteers assisting the Dutch in a campaign against Spain.

But the plot thickens, as screenwriter John Orloff explains, "There are lots of theories in the film, the main one being the Oxfordian theory which names Edward de Vere as author of the 'Shakespeare' plays. Then there's the *sub* theory—that not every Oxfordian believes—which is that Oxford and Elizabeth not only had an affair but had a child as well. This is called the Tudor Heir Theory because that child, as the theory goes, was the Earl of Southampton, the dedicatee of the sonnets. Because the voice of the sonnets is an older man talking to a younger man—like father to son—the Tudor Heir Theory answers the long mystery of why they were dedicated to Southampton."

Australian actor Xavier Samuel played Hamlet while studying at university and was most recently seen as Reily, a newborn vampire, in *The Twilight Saga: Eclipse*. He is thrilled to be back in the world of Shakespeare. ❁

Earl of Essex
ROBERT DEVEREUX
(1565 – 1601)

Sam Reid

Things began well for Robert Devereux, the Earl of Essex. His great-grandmother was Mary Boleyn (Anne Boleyn's sister), making him the queen's cousin. His god-father (later his stepfather) was Robert Dudley, the queen's long-time true love. He was well educated, studying under the best tutors available at the Cecil household (alongside his playmate Robert Cecil). And when he arrived at a somewhat aged court as a fresh, young twenty-something he won the favor of the queen and her court.

But the queen loved two types: the gallant, handsome, sporty guy fighting duels and going on adventures—which was Essex—and the serious, hard-working, staying-late-in-the-office-going-over-the-books, no-nonsense guy—that was Robert Cecil (and his father, William). Robert and Essex were rivals at court, there is no doubt. But where Robert was able to control himself, even as the queen used her "sporting" names *elf* and *pigmy*, for him, Essex was both impulsive and courageous, which led to his demise. He was insolent to the queen, disobeying her orders, and once, as the story goes, either answered her back or drew his sword on her (depending on the version).

Sir Robert Naunton described their relationship at the time, "their affections had been . . . so in and out . . . like an instrument well tuned, and lapsing to discord."

Essex was sent to Ireland in 1599 to quell an uprising but instead spent all the money and made a bad treaty, which led to his arrest and downfall. He was stripped of power (and his lucrative wine licenses), was not happy about either, and decided to rebel. In order to incite a crowd to join him, some of his supporters requested the play *Richard II*—the story of a weak monarch with bad advisors who is deposed—be performed on the eve of the uprising. Londoners, it turns out, knew better than

to rebel against Queen Elizabeth and it failed miserably. Essex was convicted of treason, and the queen broken-heartedly signed the order for his execution.

Sam Reid was still studying at drama school when he landed the role of Robert Devereux, Earl of Essex, but clearly enjoyed his on-the-job training. "This is my first film role and I've learned so much, particularly from Rhys Ifans and Vanessa Redgrave. Just watching them work has been an absolute gift."

Ever the student, he had dialect, horse riding, and fencing lessons, and spent a lot of time at the National Portrait Gallery looking over portraits from the period. "I also spent time at the Tower of London and Hampton Court, which helped me to immerse myself in the time of these characters. It was fascinating to stand in the place where Essex was actually beheaded in 1601," he says. "Regardless of what authorship theory you believe or your perspectives on Elizabeth and her reign," he continues, "*Anonymous* is a great story beautifully told. It looks at the world the author, whoever he was, was living in, his influences and inspirations—and I think that's the most fascinating thing." ✿

Ben (1572 – 1637)
JONSON
Sebastian Armesto

A month before Ben Jonson was born his father died, and so, by his own account, he was "brought up poorly." His mother married a bricklayer two years later and though he was bright in school, this London boy was not able to afford higher education and went to work for his stepfather.

In the early 1590s he got a job with an acting troupe where his writing talent clearly outshone his acting abilities. He had a talent for trouble, too. His play *The Isle of Dogs* got him jailed for "Leude and mutynous behavior," he was arrested for killing an actor in a duel, and his conversion to Catholicism in intensely Protestant England only made things worse.

His play *Every Man in His Humour*—William Shake-

speare among the cast—was his first hit. The sequel, *Every Man Out of His Humour*, played at the famous Globe theatre in 1599 and was presented at court that Christmas.

The first decade of James' rule (which began in 1603) was the most productive of Jonson's career, though trouble still followed. He was accused of treason and popperie (pushing the Pope's cause), and feuded with writers. Still he rose to become England's foremost living author, especially after the death of Shakespeare, and worked until the end of his life.

Sebastian Armesto, who plays Ben Jonson, says, "I think that this film isn't really about who wrote the Shakespeare plays as much as it's about professional and political rivalries. A lot of artists are influenced by the political atmosphere and vice versa. Whether Shakespeare's plays were designed with political intentions I don't know, but Jonson's certainly were." He goes on to say, "In the film we see Jonson before he wrote his most famous plays, he's a struggling playwright and an idealist. And like most idealists he gets a reality check. He's arrested for writing a seditious play and gets dragged into this maze of a plot by Oxford."

Thinking of the film Armesto says, "What I particularly like about *Anonymous*—beyond the fact that it's visually sumptuous—is that the story takes us through all strands of society; we see court life and street life in the same film." He continues, "Acting in this film is an absolute treat, especially doing the theatre scenes. I actually get paid to watch Mark Rylance do *Henry V*, which is an absolute pleasure." ❀

William (1564 – 1616)
SHAKESPEARE
Rafe Spall

William Shakespeare is perhaps the best known—and the most highly regarded—poet and playwright in the history of the English language. However, as you can see in Mark Twain's piece on page 21 there are not many facts known about him. He was born and raised in Stratford-upon-Avon, at eighteen he married a woman much older than him, he had three children, and at some point he moved to London to work as an actor. He wrote poems and became a playwright, though he did not give up acting. He was part owner of both Lord Chamberlain's Men—London's leading acting troupe at the time—and the Globe Theatre. He became rich enough to buy the most expensive house in Stratford. And though many of his plays were published separately during his lifetime, the First Folio, published seven years after his death, marks the first time a collection of his plays was put together.

Rafe Spall says about his character, "The William Shakespeare I'm playing is an actor first and foremost, the most famous of his day. He is from Stratford so he's provincial, working class, and he gets this incredible opportunity to take on this canon of work, the Shakespeare plays, so he runs with it. He's just a normal bloke who gets put into this extraordinary circumstance. On paper he is a bit of a baddy, but I don't see him so much being bad as being the guy who brought us the Globe. If it weren't for William Shakespeare from Stratford, there would have been no Globe theatre. He is a hero because he brought those plays to the world."

Rafe continues, "I think one of the best things about this film is that you get a fresh look at these plays. Imagine, *Hamlet*—how extraordinary it would have been—to be in the theatre watching "To be or not to be," for the first time. And these plays, like all great art, are about how they make you feel, not about the author. Great performances—acting at its very best—holds up a mirror and you think, 'Oh, I feel that, too.'"

Still he's fascinated by the Oxford premise: "This is such an extraordinary subject and I'm so proud to have a role in telling it. It is of great interest to a lot of people and it's a story that has amazing heart. It's not just academic, it's got soul." ❧

HENRY CONDELL
Mark Rylance
(1576 – 1627)

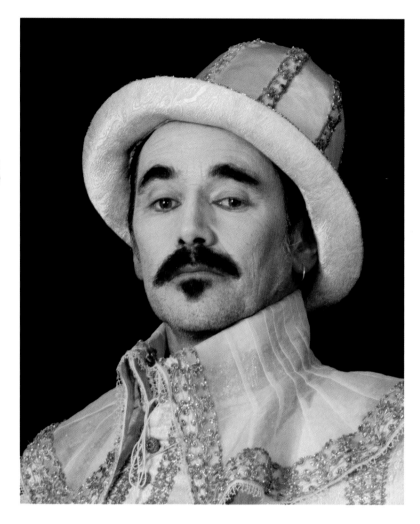

It's fitting that Mark Rylance, one of the world's most renowned Shakespearean actors, gets to play Henry Condell, one of the world's first Shakespearean actors. What's more, Rylance is playing one of the men who is responsible for compiling Shakespeare's plays. Condell, and fellow actor John Heminges, "collected them . . . without selfe-profit, or fame; onely to keepe the memory of so worthy a Friend, and Fellow alive. . . ." They, along with Shakespeare, were long-time members of the Lord Chamberlain's Men acting troupe (which became the King's Men under James I). And without this collection, known as the First Folio, which printed eighteen plays for the first time ever, it's likely there would be no *Macbeth* today.

As for who actually wrote them, "I think that there is, in reality at present, a wide candidacy for the authorship of these plays," says Rylance. "And for me the leading candidates at the moment are Sir Francis Bacon, the Earl of Oxford, and poet Mary Sidney (the Countess of Pembroke). I find them the most interesting." He clarifies his stance: "It's not that I'm anti-Stratfordian—anti-Stratfordianism is too aggressive a term for me—but the Stratford candidate, apart from lacking crucial evidence of authorship, just doesn't give me very much—though I think it's a very beautiful story."

"Furthermore," he continues, "I think a leading candidate for authorship is you, the audience member or the reader. I think that's the intention, anyway. I am Shakespeare." Rylance explains, "The author is who you choose—who you feel most reflects your understanding of the plays. I think that the author wanted the plays to be owned by all levels of society, to be understood that these plays could be written by anyone, that they would be owned by anyone. So I feel a leading candidate is somewhere inside your own mind, your own heart as a person meeting the Shakespeare work. That's what's quite interesting. And that inner author may change over your life."

As for his role in *Anonymous*, "It was a delight to work with Roland Emmerich. He is someone who is able to combine rigorously hard work with an obvious technical brilliance while maintaining—at the core—his love of telling stories."

The admiration was mutual. "The first time we did *Henry V*—with Mark Rylance on stage in our recreated theater, lit with candle and firelight—was magical for everybody," says director Roland Emmerich.

Rylance savored the opportunity, "I was thrilled to be in that smaller version of the Globe playing to that wonderful crowd of German extras, especially because the connection between the Shakespeare work and the German people is very old and wonderful. The First Folio was mentioned for the first time ever at the Frankfurt book fair in 1622."

BAFTA, Tony, and Olivier award winner Mark Rylance was the first Artistic Director of the current incarnation of Shakespeare's Globe Theatre. In 2007 he wrote the play *I Am Shakespeare*, which grew from his obsession with being nearer to artists he admires, whoever they turn out to be. ❧

PROLOGUE
Derek Jacobi

Shakespeare is the Elizabethan age," says stage and screen legend Derek Jacobi. He continues, "He encapsulated, in the plays, in the poems, so much of the ethos of that time. And it's all there. The passion, the adventure, the discovery, the questioning, the expansion of man's thought and reach. They're all in those works. And we need—I need—to find out who this person was."

In *Anonymous*, he plays prologue to the Shakespeare authorship question itself, and says, "It feels great to be introducing the question to a worldwide audience. When I was asked to do it my first thought was, 'Well, at last. This is a big-time movie which is presenting the argument, presenting the problem.' The movie then goes on into other spheres, but at least the problem is stated. No solution is given. But we are saying, 'Have you, ladies and gentlemen, ever thought that it wasn't the man from Stratford?'"

"The killer question, of course," he says, "is, 'who?' I think most probably it's de Vere. Whether single-handedly I'm not sure. But, de Vere with his background of aristocracy, his legal background, his musical background. The works are from somebody who didn't just acquire bits of knowledge in the tavern from sailors or from someone who worked in a library for a year. No, this is much deeper than that. It is a much broader, educative idea that this man from a very young age was steeped in culture. And that is manifest in practically every line he wrote."

He explains his passion for the topic: "After millions of words, after 400 years of research, thinking about him, writing about it, we still don't know anything. Nothing. Something like eighty-two facts—I mean, known facts—mainly legal, judicial. But the canvas is blank. And this is why for me the authorship question is so important. I need to put some colors in there. I need to fill it out."

His conclusion, "It is the best who-done-it in the world."

BAFTA, Tony, and Emmy Award winner, Jacobi recently appeared as the Archbishop of Canterbury in *The King's Speech* and is probably best known for playing the title role in the 1976 BBC TV miniseries *I Claudius*. ❦

The play's the thing . . . wherein I'll

tch the conscience of the king.

The Soul of
THE SCRIPT

John Orloff

Why had no one told me this?

That was my first thought when, twenty years ago, I first learned of Edward de Vere and the Shakespeare authorship question. My second thought was—what a fantastic film this would make. It had everything: murder, sex, lies, betrayal. Truly, the stuff of a Shakespearean drama.

But I was a twenty-five-year-old American who had only written a script or two in film school at UCLA. Who was I to write actual dialogue for William Shakespeare, much less dare suggest he wasn't the true author?

And so instead, I focused on a soul-crushing career in advertising.

But the story of Edward de Vere haunted me, and I read exhaustively on the subject. I talked about it a dinner parties (where I got into more than a few arguments). I talked about it incessantly to my then-girlfriend (and now wife). I talked about it to whoever would listen.

So much so that about fifteen years ago, my wife finally said to me: "Why don't you just write the damn thing already? If it's terrible, you don't have to show it to anyone."

OPPOSITE: *Rhys Ifans as Edward de Vere, the 17th Earl of Oxford.*

And I realized she was right. I hated working in advertising, and I had always dreamed of making films . . . but how to write it? How to take such a controversial topic and such a complex life as Edward de Vere's and turn it into a two-hour film?

Well, a writer's best friend is procrastination, so more research was in order. Now this was in the infancy of the Internet, so no help was to be had there. Instead, I went to bookstores and libraries. I read every book I could find about Elizabethan England. Every book about William Cecil, Robert Cecil, Queen Elizabeth. Every book about Tudor stagecraft, about life "Bankside." And of course, I had to re-read as many of the plays and poems as I could.

But still, I couldn't find my "in" to the story. There was so much. Too much! Should it be set in the present, and be a hunt to find the true author? Or should it be a classic, cradle-to-grave bio-pic? Neither of those felt right.

And then, in reading the works of Shakespeare's contemporary Ben Jonson, I found something that sparked an idea. In several works, Jonson makes clear his loathing for Shakespeare. In one famous poem he lambastes

ABOVE: *Screenwriter John Orloff (center).*
RIGHT: *Rafe Spall as William Shakespeare.*

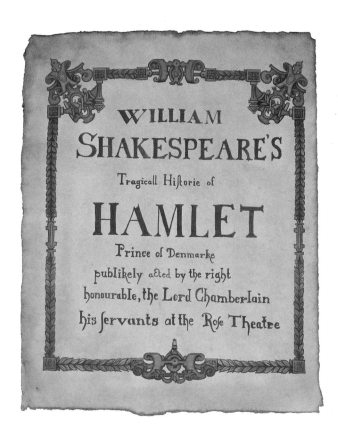

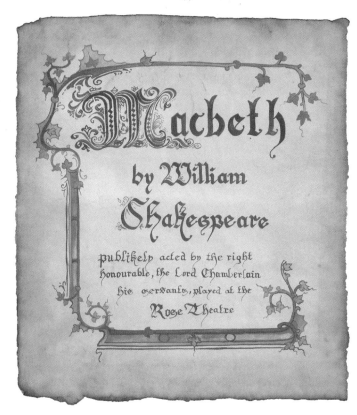

Shakespeare as "poet-ape," while in one of his plays, Jonson famously lampoons him as a buffoon, whose crest contains a "boar without a head" (de Vere's family symbol was the boar), and whose motto was "Not Without Mustard!" (Shakespeare's actual motto was "Not Without Right").

But in the preface to the First Folio, Jonson calls Shakespeare the "Soul of the Age," and proclaims him the greatest poet since the Ancient Greeks. That struck me as inconsistent. So, I thought, what if Jonson were talking about two different people? One, the true poet, the "Soul of the Age," and the other, just a poet-ape, a fraud, a charlatan? What if Ben Jonson... knew the truth?

Suddenly, I had my "in." The young and struggling playwright Ben Jonson—a character I could definitely relate to—would guide us through the film. The Earl of Oxford would approach Jonson, not Shakespeare, to be his "beard," but Jonson, wanting to achieve immortality by his own pen, would naturally demur, leaving a vacuum that the ambitious actor Will Shakespeare would happily fill. Now that's the foundation of a film!

And after two years of part-time writing and many, many wrong turns, I finished a first draft. I called it "Soul

of the Age." And two months later, *Shakespeare in Love* came out. And trust me, no one wanted to make another Shakespeare movie. So the script sat on the shelf. For eight years or so.

Until I met the unlikeliest of heroes: Roland Emmerich. I was in his office to talk about *The Day After Tomorrow*, and, as often happens in these meetings, I started to talk about "Soul of the Age." His eyes instantly lit up. He wanted to read it.

And read it he did. He optioned it a week later, and soon became as obsessed with the story as I was. He read as many books as he could find on the subject as well. And in the eight years since I had originally written "Soul of the Age," there had been many more books published with new research and new ideas.

And so Roland approached me with a rather radical idea: What if we inserted the Succession Crisis into the film? At the end of her reign, Elizabeth refused to name an heir, which caused all sorts of jockeying in the Court. But theories had been presented that de Vere and Elizabeth had had an affair early in her reign, and some have even suggested they had had a child, a male who was raised as the Earl of Southampton (the dedicatee of Shakespeare's

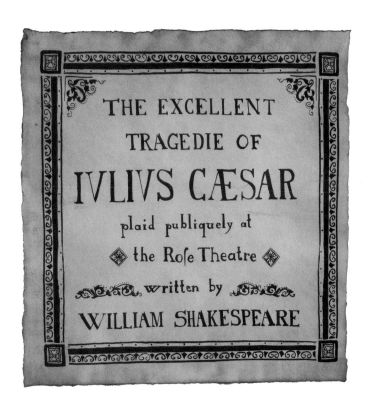

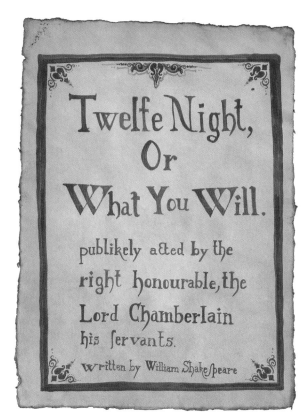

Venus and Adonis, and the possible "fair youth" of the sonnets). And also, if true, an heir.

Now none of this was in "Soul of the Age," and I could see in Roland's eyes he was quite worried what my reaction would be—no doubt concerned that I would think he wanted to ruin my "perfect" script. I took a deep breath, considered it for two seconds, and thought, Oh my God, what a brilliant idea!

Roland wanted to propel a pretty good script into a whole new dimension of dramatic possibility. Now I wasn't so sure what I thought of this notion as history, but I knew it was possible (Virgin Queen? Really?). And suddenly, a little film about art and jealousy and the triumph of the creative spirit became a much bigger film about the intersection of art and politics, and whether the pen is indeed mightier than the sword. Shakespearean stuff indeed.

So began what for me has been one of the most exciting collaborations I have ever experienced. Working in Roland's living room and kitchen, day after day, ripping my script apart in order to build it anew. Do we put in the Essex Rebellion? How? Do we show Marlowe murdered? By whom? When does the audience figure out who Elizabeth and de Vere's son actually is? Early? Late?

We tried it all different ways. Draft after draft. I lost count. Ten . . . twenty . . . thirty. But each draft was getting better, closer. But it took years to get it to a place where we thought we had the right balance of characters, of themes, of plots.

Finally, eight years or so after I first met Roland, I found myself on the Babelsberg Stages in Potsdam, Germany, watching hundreds of talented people bringing their own unique gifts to my twenty-year-old dream. Roland had assembled an amazing group of people, both in front of the camera and behind it. There were no "easy" days, all of them eternally long, but all of them incredibly rewarding.

And so it seems it will take the collaboration of these many artists to let others learn of the Shakespeare authorship question. Some members of our audience may be convinced, others not, but all will be transported in time to witness Elizabethan England as never seen before, and hopefully all will see our celebration of one man's genius, whoever he may have been. ❧

ABOVE: *Prop play posters created by Jan Jericho.*

65

The Play Begins...

EXT/INT. THE ROSE THEATRE

> **POLE** (*to a soldier*)
> Torch it.

The soldier hesitates.

> **POLE** (*cont'd*)
> Torch it! All of you!

The soldiers obey, lighting fire to the walls, the galleries, the columns as— Jonson gasps in horror. Desperate— he spies an open metal box nearby filled with unused fireworks.

He tosses the fireworks out of the box— and then places the bound manuscripts in their place, then closes the box. Then— he grabs a nearby rapier as— FLAMES —begin to take hold everywhere: the columns at the front of the stage. . . the trompe-l'oeil walls. . . the seating galleries. . . the columns. . . A trap door opens center-stage, and Jonson jumps out, the rapier in his right hand, ready for a fight. But— three soldiers jump onto the stage, pikes ready.

Jonson—no fool—turns and runs for the other end of the stage— but then runs smack into four other soldiers! Bollocks! Jonson turns this way and that— nowhere to run— grins wryly, drops his sword. Raises his hands in surrender.

EXT. THE ROSE THEATRE–NIGHT

Jonson, his hands tied behind him, is pushed through the door, Pole following.

A small crowd of actors, whores, etc., watch the theatre burn. The guards have to push their way through them.

INSERT

The fire reaches the fireworks below the theatre's stage, and— BACK TO SCENE— the sound of fireworks exploding makes Jonson turn and see:

THE THEATRE

Timbers CRASH and fireworks EXPLODE over the theatre.

THE ROSE & THE GLOBE

Elizabethan acting companies originally staged their performances in inn yards, college halls, or private houses (and of course at court), and the Rose was only the fifth purpose-built theatre to exist in London. It was built in Bankside, an area already rich in entertainments, ranging from brothels to bear-baiting arenas.

Its rival, the Globe, arrived in 1599, and along with the Swan, swiftly put the Rose out of business. Abandoned by 1606 it completely vanished from the map until 1989 when it turned up under a demolished building.

The Globe came about due to a landlord-tenant dispute. Having lost their lease, the Lord Chamberlain's Men literally took their theatre (called the Theatre), which they owned, piece by piece, across the Thames and built the Globe. To cover the costs, owners Cuthbert Burbage and his brother, famed actor Richard, offered shares—one of which Will Shakespeare bought. It thrived for fourteen years until flaming debris shot from a cannon during a performance of *Henry VIII* got caught in the thatch. It was rebuilt with a tile roof but finally closed under the Puritans in 1642.

Nine years earlier

EXT. ROSE THEATRE/BANKSIDE LONDON–CONTINUOUS

The Rose towers above the nearby buildings "Bankside" (the part of London that houses the theatres, whorehouses, etc.).

SOUTHAMPTON (O.S.)
Well?

Two men walk towards the theatre. Edward de Vere (47), the Earl of Oxford, an intensely handsome man. His clothes have seen better days.

His companion is Henry Wriothesley, Earl of Southampton (22). Blonde, attractive, a bit of a pretty boy—and extremely enthusiastic.

SOUTHAMPTON (cont'd)
Wonderful, isn't it?

OXFORD (frowning slightly)
Well, it's certainly . . . big.

SOUTHAMPTON
I promise you, Edward, you've seen nothing like it before! Nothing!

INT. CHANGING ROOMS/ESSEX HOUSE–DAY

Southampton and Essex are dressing out of their tennis clothes and into their normal clothes, assisted by two valets.

ESSEX *(to the valets)*
Leave us. *(they exit)* Henry . . . Some of my men have . . . intercepted . . . some of William Cecil's recent correspondence with King James of Scotland . . .

Southampton pauses in clothing himself. This is serious.

ESSEX *(cont'd)*
Cecil's all but promising him the throne . . .

SOUTHAMPTON
To James? Elizabeth would never agree to—

ESSEX
Elizabeth is old. Ill. Not of her old mind. Sometimes she doesn't even recognize me. And yet, still she refuses to name an heir.

SOUTHAMPTON
But a Scotsman? On the Tudor throne?

ESSEX
You are not in the Privy Council. Elizabeth does everything the Cecils wish of her. Everything!

INT. CECIL HOUSE–GREAT HALL–DUSK

A dwarf enters, followed by dancing fairies, actors swirling sparklers, and musicians playing music.

Elizabeth's rheumy eyes widen in complete delight, a smile of total jubilation crosses her face.

Robert Cecil, on the other hand, looks horrified.

> **ELIZABETH**
> Are you this gift, my precious little man?

> **DWARF**
> No, no, my most majestic majesty. I am a free man. My gift is a play, majesty.

> **ELIZABETH**
> A play?

The dwarf bows his assent.

> **ROBERT CECIL** (to the Dwarf)
> Plays are the work of the devil, born from a cesspool of plague, whoredom, thievery, fornication, and heresy. You may tell your master that her majesty—

> **ESSEX** (interrupting)
> —Will gladly accept your gift.

Robert Cecil turns to Essex, shocked.

> **ESSEX** (cont'd) (to Elizabeth)
> Of course that is if you so desire, majesty. (to Robert Cecil) The choice is her majesty's to make, not yours. Is that not so, Sir Robert?

Robert frowns as Elizabeth looks around, unsure of the political tides around her. Then—

> **ELIZABETH** (to the dwarf)
> Comedy? Or tragedy?

> **DWARF**
> Comedy, majesty.

> **ELIZABETH** (delighted)
> A comedy! (beat) By whom?

> **DWARF**
> By . . . Anonymous, your majesty . . .

> **ELIZABETH**
> Anonymous . . .? (then) Oh, but I do so admire his verse . . .

37 years earlier

INT. HEDINGHAM CASTLE–KITCHEN

YOUNG ELIZABETH (O.S.)
Ah! There he is.

Young Elizabeth and her senior Court, including William Cecil and John de Vere, have entered.

Boy Oxford bows deeply.

YOUNG ELIZABETH (cont'd)
Your father tells me you wrote this evening's play yourself.

Boy Oxford glances at his father—should he answer directly? His father nods.

BOY OXFORD
I did indeed, your majesty.

INT. RICHMOND PALACE–RECEIVING CHAMBER–NIGHT

A door SLAMS open, and Young Elizabeth and Young Oxford dash in, ripping each others clothes off in the fireplace-lit room.

Young Elizabeth gently pushes Young Oxford towards her throne . . . She kisses him. Then begin to make love. On the throne.

DISSOLVE TO: LATER

Postcoital, the fire still lit. Young Elizabeth is half asleep, half awake, nestled in furs in front of the fireplace . . . much like Titania in *Midsummer Night's Dream* . . .

Young Oxford watches her as she stirs and wakes. She smiles at him.

YOUNG ELIZABETH
I can't decide. Are you Prince Hal . . .? Or Romeo? No. Benedick, maybe . . .? No— (*smiles*) —Puck

YOUNG OXFORD (*smiles*)
Puck?

YOUNG ELIZABETH
Yes, Puck!

She's only teasing.

YOUNG OXFORD
Ah, but Puck would never fight for you in the Netherlands . . .

YOUNG ELIZABETH (*surprised, smiles*)
The Netherlands?

But then she realizes he's serious, and the smile vanishes.

YOUNG OXFORD
Well, why not? It's an open secret on the continent that you support the rebels against Spain— and that you are commissioning Englishmen to help their cause. Spain's loss is England's gain, is it not?

Her eyes narrow as she studies his face.

YOUNG ELIZABETH
Is this why you bedded me? For a commission?

YOUNG OXFORD
No. No— of course not— I—

She stands, wrapped in her sheets, furious at the thought of once more being used.

YOUNG ELIZABETH
Leave me. Leave at once!

30 years later

EXT. OXFORD STONE–GARDEN–DAY

Oxford smells the rose, inhaling its essence. Then he turns and sees Francesco escorting Ben Jonson towards him.

Before they reach him he glances at his wife Anne De Vere (40's) who sits in the distance knitting with one of their daughter's, Bridget (17).

Jonson is quite uncomfortable to be at such a grand place. Jonson clears his throat.

> JONSON
>
> My lord . . .

> OXFORD
>
> The Tudor rose. The most beautiful of flowers, don't you think?

> JONSON
>
> It looks to me to have quite a number of thorns, my lord.

> OXFORD
>
> So it does. So it does.

> JONSON
>
> I am told, my lord, that I owe my freedom to you.

> OXFORD
>
> That is true. And it was quite hard to come by. One does not cross my father-in-law lightly.

Jonson doesn't know who he is talking about.

> OXFORD (cont'd)
>
> Lord William Cecil. I have the questionable distinction of being married to his only daughter.

Oxford looks over to his wife who watches them suspiciously. He begins to walk away forcing Jonson and Francesco to follow.

> OXFORD (cont'd)
>
> It did, however, serve as helpful when I wrote to your jailers to release you in my father-in-law's name.

Jonson suddenly looks worried and turns and looks back to Anne.

> JONSON (in a panicked whisper)
>
> My lord—I'm sorry, does that mean my release is not officially sanctioned?

> OXFORD
>
> Don't be an idiot Jonson, of course it wasn't. (beat) But you are free, are you not?

They have come to an entrance to a garden maze and Anne watches them as they disappear into the maze.

EXT. MAZE–DAY

Oxford turns to Jonson.

> OXFORD
>
> I enjoyed your little comedy last week, Jonson. You have potential, great potential.

> JONSON
>
> Thank you, my lord.

> OXFORD
>
> But its politics did seem to have quite an effect on the Tower. My

father-in-law's men felt it quite seditious.

> JONSON
>
> Politics? My play had nothing to do with politics! It was just a simple comedy—

> OXFORD
>
> That showed your betters as fools who go through life barely managing to get food from plate to mouth, were it not for the cleverness of their servants. (beat) All art is political, Jonson. Otherwise it would just be decoration. And all artists have something to say, otherwise . . . they'd make shoes. And you're not a cobbler, are you, Jonson?

As they enter the center of the maze, Oxford turns to his servant.

> OXFORD (cont'd) (nods)
>
> Francesco.

Francesco steps forward and hands Jonson a leather bound manuscript. Jonson looks at it confused and opens it.

> JONSON
>
> A play, my lord?

> OXFORD
>
> One you shall stage Bankside.

> JONSON
>
> Stage?

> OXFORD
>
> Under your name.

> JONSON
>
> My name, my lord?

> OXFORD
>
> I can't very well use my name, can I? I'm the seventeenth Earl of Oxford. The Lord Great Chamberlain of England, Viscount Bolebec, Lord Escales, Sandford and Badlesmere, etc, etc. No. I have a . . . reputation to protect. In my world, one does not write plays, Jonson. People like you do.

**INT. THE MERMAID'S TAVERN–
NIGHT**

Shakespeare is perusing the
manuscript. Some of the actors
from the Rose are in the BG.

      SHAKESPEARE
You know, it's actually not
half bad. . .

Jonson takes a swig of ale, then—

      JONSON
Not half—?! You're an actor, what
in God's name do you know about
writing?! He's an amateur, Will,
a complete and utter amateur.
Last week gardening, this
week playwrighting, next week
hawking. *(takes another swig)*
No. I won't do it. It would be an
affront against the Muses. . .

      SHAKESPEARE *(smiles)*
Well we musn't offend the muses,
whatever we do. *(thinks, then)*
How much money did you say he
gave you?

      JONSON
What, you think my name can
be bought, if the number's great
enough, do you?

Shakespeare smiles enigmatically.

      SHAKESPEARE
No, not at all. . . I think we should
keep your good name quite intact,
thank you very much.

Digestive cheese, and fruit
there sure will bee;
But that, which most doth
take my Muse, and mee,
Is a pure cup of rich
Canary-wine,
Which is the Mermaid's,
now, but shall be mine.

—*Inviting a Friend to Supper*
by Ben Jonson

EXT/INT. ROSE THEATRE–DAY

Southampton arrives at the theatre. He jumps off his horse, and hurries

INTO THE STAIRWELL

jumping two steps at a time. We hear the sound of applause. The play is now over. Southampton hurries into

OXFORD'S BOX

He sees Oxford, who is applauding. All the actors of the play are taking their bows.

> **SOUTHAMPTON**
> William Cecil's convinced the Queen that only Essex can save Ireland from the Revolt.

Oxford processes this.

> **SOUTHAMPTON** (cont'd)
> I've pledged to go with him, Edward. We sail in an hour.

> **OXFORD**
> Henry—

> **SOUTHAMPTON**
> I ask for your blessing, Edward.

> **OXFORD**
> I can't give it to you.

IN THE GALLERIES

> **NASHE**
> I for one wish to see this anonymous colleague of ours. (stands) Playwright! Playwright!!

Marlowe and others join in. And—

BACKSTAGE

Shakespeare, standing next to a small table of props, quickly dips his fingers in an inkwell to make them stained. He grabs a large feathered quill and tucks a piece of parchment under his arm, then hurries—

ON STAGE

—where he bows deeply, loving the adulation.

INT. OXFORD STONE–STUDY–DAY

The multi-arched ceiling is painted blue with gold stars. Globes—both terrestrial and astral—abound.

Jonson stands in front of a very angry Oxford.

> **OXFORD**
> An actor for god's sake?

> **JONSON**
> My lord, I thought that—

> **OXFORD**
> You presumed to think? On my behalf? Whatever made you believe you had that prerogative?

A beat. Jonson is a bit afraid.

> **JONSON**
> My lord, your voice is completely different than mine. My, my, my characters are—

> **OXFORD**
> Voice? You have no voice! That's why I chose you! *(beat, softer)* You at least kept my name from him?

Jonson NODS.

> **OXFORD** *(cont'd)*
> And will continue to do so?

Oxford studies him, believes him. Then he opens a cabinet.

In it, manuscript after manuscript are stacked. Jonson looks behind him, stunned by the number.

Oxford looks up and down the cabinet. He pulls one out, decides no, and puts it back, looking for just the right one . . . He pulls another out, then hands it to Jonson.

> **OXFORD** *(cont'd)*
> A romantic tragedy. In iambic pentameter.

> **JONSON** *(amazed)*
> All, my lord? Is that possible?

> **OXFORD**
> Of course it is!

EXT. LONDON BRIDGE–DAY

Shakespeare and Jonson are walking along London Bridge—the only bridge that spanned the Thames at the time, it is a street lined with multi-storied buildings—almost like a mall.

Shakespeare carries and reads from a manuscript of *Romeo and Juliet*.

> SHAKESPEARE
> "From ancient grudge break
>   to new mutiny,
> Where civil blood makes civil
>   hands unclean." *(no longer reading)*
> Incredible!! The whole bloody thing
> in verse?!

> JONSON *(nonchalant)*
> It's really not that difficult, if you try.

> SHAKESPEARE
> And have you ever tried?

Jonson gives him a sharp look, and pauses to pick some onions from a stand.

Shakespeare notices a buxom blonde woman selling apples at the next stand.

> SHAKESPEARE *(cont'd)*
> *(performing for the Blonde)*
> "But soft, what light through
> yonder window breaks?
> It is the east, and Juliet is the sun.
> Arise, fair sun, and kill the
>   envious moon,

Who is already sick and pale
  with grief,
That thou her maid art far more
  fair than she."

The Buxom Blonde smiles at Shakespeare seductively.

> SHAKESPEARE *(cont'd) (to Jonson)*
> I'll have little trouble parting
> the legs of barmaids after that
> performance!

> JONSON
> You can't play Romeo.

Jonson leaves the stall, and continues down the street. Shakespeare hesitates, then gives the girl a dazzling smile. She smiles back, then Shakespeare runs after Jonson.

> SHAKESPEARE *(to Jonson)*
> Why not? I won't let that oaf
> Spencer have another go at
> one of my roles. No— only Will
> Shakespeare can pump the life
> into Romeo's veins. *(grins at another
> passing girl)* And his cod piece!
> *(beat, desperate)* Ben— Ben! I'm an
> actor, every inch of me, down to my
> very toes . . . I want—no, I need,
> crave—to act. I can't just idle the
> day by with—

> JONSON
> So bloody well act like a writer! And
> for God's sake, keep off the stage.
> Writers don't have time to act.

THE MERMAID WITS

The Mermaid Tavern, located in Cheapside at the corner of Friday and Bread Streets (just east of St. Paul's Cathedral), is where a group of literary men met the first Friday of each month to discuss—sometimes heatedly—politics, religion, and literature. Known as The Mermaid Wits (or The Friday Street Club), they also, from time to time, amused themselves by inventing libelous and scurrilous verses. Among this group of poets, playwrights, and actors were Sir Walter Raleigh (sometimes said to have started the club), Thomas Nashe, Christopher Marlowe, William Shakespeare, William Shake-

Jonson. (Pictured above: Tony Way as Nashe, Trystan Gravelle as Marlowe, Rafe Spall as Shakespeare, Roberts Emms as Dekker and Sebastian Armesto as Jonson.)

Historian Thomas Fuller said, "Many were the wit-combats betwixt him (Shakespeare) and Ben Jonson . . . Jonson was built far higher in learning . . . *solid* but *slow* in his performances. Shakespeare lesser in *bulk* . . . could *turn with all tides*, and take advantage of *all winds*, by the quickness of his wit and invention."

The tavern, along with 13,000 other buildings in London, burned down in the Great Fire of 1666.

INT. THE MERMAID'S TAVERN DAY

Jonson, Marlowe, Dekker and Nashe sit silently at a table, mugs of ale in hand. Having just returned from *Romeo and Juliet*, all are a bit in shock. The actors from the performance are there as well in the BG.

    MARLOWE *(to Nashe)*
Do what?

    NASHE *(a little drunk)*
A play in iambic, in iambic pen . . . in-bic-pentameter. It's not that hard.

    JONSON
Think you so? Have you ever tried?

    NASHE
Of course not. But I could if I wanted . . .

    DEKKER
It wasn't all in verse.

    NASHE
Ha! See! Even easier!

Shakespeare enters and makes a bee line for them.

    SHAKESPEARE *(excited)*
Henslowe wants *Romeo* to run a fortnight. *(unbelievable*

A round for everybody! Innkeeper!! *(no response)* Billy!!!

And Shakespeare goes over to the bar.

    NASHE
A fortnight?

    DEKKER
The maids love the romantic tragedies.

    MARLOWE
Precisely why I avoid them.

    NASHE
Aw, well. No worries. A one-trick pony. He'll never be

INT. CECIL HOUSE–WILLIAM CECIL'S STUDY–DAY

Robert Cecil is furious, pacing back and forth in front of William Cecil, who sits behind a large wooden desk.

William Cecil is pale and sweaty— he is deathly ill, and sits in a wooden chair with small spoked wheels attached to the legs—sort of an Elizabethan wheelchair.

William Cecil pushes a hidden button on the side of his desk—a spring loaded secret drawer pops open. Robert Cecil has never seen it before.

Cecil produces a folded piece of parchment from the drawer, offers it to Robert Cecil.

> **WILLIAM CECIL** *(cont'd)*
> From King James of Scotland.

Robert Cecil looks surprised.

INT. CECIL HOUSE–HALLWAY– MOMENTS LATER

Robert Cecil is pushing William Cecil in his wheelchair. They are completely alone.

> **WILLIAM CECIL**
> James knows of the Queen's affection for Essex . . . and the rumors of his birth. He is justly concerned. *(beat)* You will reply to him.

> **ROBERT CECIL**
> I will reply to him?

> **WILLIAM CECIL**
> I am dying, Robert— *(before Robert can protest)* We both know this to be true. And I will not witness the next coronation.

INT. CECIL HOUSE–WILLIAM CECIL'S BEDROOM–MOMENTS LATER

Robert Cecil wheels his father in.

> **WILLIAM CECIL**
> Help me to my bed, my son. *(Robert Cecil does so)* If we are to secure your place at the side of the next king, you must get that king his throne, not I.

A beat as this registers on Robert Cecil.

WILLIAM CECIL *(cont'd)*
You will write to James that I am gravely ill, but that all is in hand. Much of the Privy Council has already secretly agreed to his ascension to the English throne due to your tireless, but secret, entreaties on his behalf. *(beat)*

And then tell him Essex will not return from Ireland alive.

Robert Cecil looks surprised.

WILLIAM CECIL *(cont'd)*
This is how kings are made, Robert. So it was with Elizabeth, and so it shall ever be. There were many rival claims to her throne, but none survived to make their claim. James must know that you will do the same for him, and he will reward you for it. *(beat)* But we must do one thing more . . .

William Cecil has a coughing fit—reaches for a glass vial of medicine at his bedside— takes it.

WILLIAM CECIL *(cont'd)*
Like Essex, Edward must be removed.

ROBERT CECIL *(confused)*
Edward?

William Cecil is slowly falling asleep . . .

WILLIAM CECIL
He uses the tools at his disposal, as we use the tools at ours. But ours will win . . . as they always have.

ROBERT CECIL *(more confused)*
I— I don't understand, father. What does Edward—

WILLIAM CECIL
Edward seeks what we seek. To choose the next King.

**INT. WHITEHALL PALACE–OLD
ELIZABETH'S BEDROOM–DUSK**

Elizabeth is looking out the window.
It's raining outside. She is NOT
wearing her wig, not much make-up,
and looks quite . . . odd.

Robert Cecil enters.

> **ELIZABETH** *(turns)*
> You find me disgusting, don't you?
> Repugnant. Wrinkled?

> **ROBERT CECIL**
> You, you are the sun, majesty. The
> glory of—

> **ELIZABETH**
> Liar!

Robert Cecil shuts his mouth.

> **ELIZABETH** *(cont'd)*
> Is it so hard to believe that once I
> was young? That I was . . . beauti-
> ful? Your father knew me as such
> . . . *(beat)* You have read the book?

She doesn't have to say which one.
Robert Cecil sees a copy of *Venus and
Adonis* on a table. He NODS.

> **ELIZABETH** *(cont'd)*
> He writes to me. To remind me of
> that beauty. That love. How I . . .
> took him. How I . . . adored him . . .

Robert Cecil knows to be silent. She
looks out the window.

> **ELIZABETH** *(cont'd) (throaty, sexually)*
> Graze on my lips; and if
> those hills be dry,
> Stray lower, where the pleasant
> fountains lie . . .

She smiles seductively, transported
in time.

> **ELIZABETH** *(cont'd)*
> I've been foolish. Proud. Yes. Too
> proud. Gloriana . . . The Virgin
> Queen . . . A statue. Bloodless. *(beat)*
> "Thou wast begot; to beget is
> thy duty.
> By law of nature thou art bound
> to breed, That thine may live
> when thou thyself art dead" . . .
> *(beat)*
> Your father told you of the child?

(beat.)

> **ROBERT CECIL** *(hint of a smile)*
> Which one, your majesty?

Elizabeth's eyes flare in anger for an
instant, then she regains composure.

> **ELIZABETH**
> His. Mine. He still lives?

Robert Cecil nods.

> **ELIZABETH** *(cont'd)*
> He was well placed? A nobleman?

> **ROBERT CECIL** *(hesitates)*
> Yes . . . your majesty.

> **ELIZABETH**
> Who?

Robert Cecil hesitates.

> **ELIZABETH** *(cont'd)*
> I am your Queen! Now who is
> my son!!?

> **ROBERT CECIL**
> His grace, the Earl of . . .
> Southampton, your majesty.

SWITCHING RICHARDS

An interesting footnote to the Essex rebellion (1601) is that in an attempt to generate support for the uprising, a follower of the Earl of Essex paid Shakespeare's acting company (the Lord Chamberlain's Men) to put on a performance of *Richard II*. The play shows Henry Bolingbroke, cousin to Richard II, removing Richard from the throne and setting himself up as king. The play was performed the day before the rebellion, but failed to generate the hoped-for popular backing for Essex. With little support, he retreated to Essex House before surrendering to authorities. At the trial, Augustine Phillips, a member of the troupe, explained that they knew nothing about the rebellion and had only performed the old and "out of use" play because they had been paid 40 shillings more than their usual rate. Ultimately the Lord Chamberlain's Men didn't suffer any serious consequences, and they even performed for Queen Elizabeth the day before Essex was executed.

In the movie, the performance of *Richard II* is replaced with *Richard III* to suggest a connection between the villainous hunchbacked King Richard III and the ill-shaped Robert Cecil, the Queen's closest advisor.

EXT. BANKSIDE LONDON–DAY

The crowd pours through Bankside, growing in numbers as more people come out of taverns, whore-houses, etc . . .

A shop-owner comes out of his store, confused. Another MAN grabs him.

> MAN
> To Essex! And then to the Queen!
> (*joins in the chanting*) Ess-ex! Ess-ex!

The shop-owner begins to get the spirit of the mob.

EXT. LONDON BRIDGE–DAY

If anything, the crowd is twice the size it was moments ago. They head down the shop-lined bridge, full of bravado.

Jonson is in the middle of the uncontrolled mob. He spots Francesco nearby.

WIDER

The mob has to slow down on the bridge. There is not much room.

And then it happens!

We are at the front of the mob, when the first soldiers appear and pull down the tarps revealing the cannons.

People scream as an Officer appears and—

> OFFICER
> Fire!

INT. OXFORD STONE–OXFORD'S BEDROOM–CONTINUOUS

Oxford, in bed, looks quite ill, sweat covering his brow.

He furiously writes on a small tablet on his lap. He holds up his hand for silence as Jonson enters, the doctor following behind him.

> **OXFORD**
> Thank you, doctor.

The doctor exits.

> **OXFORD** (cont'd)
> Come over here, Jonson . . .

He points to a chair by the bed. When Jonson sits down he notices a big pile of manuscripts by the side of the bed.

> **OXFORD** (cont'd)
> Did you know, Jonson, that my family can trace its peerage farther back than any family in the kingdom? We fought at Crecy. At Bosworth Field. At Agincourt. (beat) I inherited my Earldom as one of the wealthiest men ever to breathe English air . . . and at last breath, I shall be one of the poorest.

Jonson looks on sadly.

> **OXFORD** (cont'd)
> Never a voice in government. Never a sword raised in glorious battle. No immortal deeds for my heirs to

know me by. (beat) Words, merely words, are to be my legacy . . . (beat) You alone watch my plays and know them as mine. When I hear the applause, the cheering, of the audience, all those hands clapping, they are celebrating . . . another man. But in that cacophony of sounds, I strained to hear the sound of two hands only. Yours. (beat) But heard them, I never did.

Jonson stares at him.

> **OXFORD** (cont'd)
> Death takes away all pretense and demands honesty from its target. You, you have never told me . . . never told me what you thought of my work . . .

To answer is not an easy task for Jonson's ego. He hesitates.

> **JONSON** (almost a whisper)
> I find . . . your words . . . the most wondrous ever heard on our stage. On any stage . . . Ever.

The two men now looking each other in the eye.

> **JONSON** (cont'd) (sotto)
> You are the soul of the age . . .

Oxford smiles at the thought of it. Then—

> **OXFORD**
> Promise me . . . promise me, Jonson, that you will keep our secret safe. That you won't expose Shakespeare . . .

> **JONSON**
> My lord?

> **OXFORD**
> I have seen it in your face . . . He vexes you. How could he not? But he is not your burden. He is mine.

Then he nods to the manuscripts by his side.

> **OXFORD** (cont'd)
> All my writings. The plays, the sonnets . . . Keep them safe. Keep them from my family. From the Cecils. Wait a few years, and then, publish them.

All the world's a stage, and all the men

ACT IV
THE THEATRE
...nd women merely players.

A Midwinter
DAY'S DREAM

Tamara Harvey
Theatre Scenes Director

On a freezing, grey day in February, I followed Director Roland Emmerich, Production Designer Sebastian Krawinkel, First Assistant Director Chris Doll, and a shivering group of various others bundled up in hats and scarves through what would become the huge wooden doors of our Rose (and later Globe) Theatre. When I'd been in Berlin less than two months earlier, the builders hadn't even broken ground on the site. The Globe Theatre on London's South Bank took over twenty years and an untold number of expert opinions to be built. How could this thing, that had been designed and then thrown up in a matter of months, possibly be the space it needed to be in order to convey the magic of these Elizabethan playhouses, in order to convey the power of the stories that needed to be told?

And then I stepped through the open doorway. And there it was. A wooden O. Incomplete, half its stage missing, unpainted, and yet . . . and yet . . . it was perfect; a living, breathing theatre waiting for players and audience to gather in. And suddenly I realized it didn't matter whether the dimensions were historically accurate or whether we were leaving the balustrades unpainted when we're pretty certain that they were highly decorated in Shakespeare's day; it didn't matter that the programmes we were going to use to tell our story were anachronistic or that the plays were not in what we believe to have been the chronological order of their first performances. Suddenly the only thing that mattered is that we had the chance to tell stories in this beautiful new theatre in which the fundamentals would be true. There would be actors on the stage, audiences encircling them in the yard and in the galleries and everyone would be in the same light so

ABOVE: *Aerial view of the Rose theatre set.*
RIGHT: *(from left to right) Tamara Harvey, Roland Emmerich, and actor Mark Rylance.*

that everything—every emotion, every witticism, every twist in the plot, every heartfelt cry—would be shared.

Whoever wrote these plays did so with the knowledge that stories, if told with heart and with truth, have the power to move people—to laughter, to tears and sometimes, just sometimes, to action. And theatre, at the moment in history when our story is told, was one of the few forums in which stories could be told. There was no television, no film, no radio; there weren't even any newspapers. There certainly wasn't an Internet and books were precious and rare. And yet for a penny, you could walk into a theatre with three thousand others and hear a new story, or even an old story told in a new way, for many of the plays were retelling old tales.

Is this the way that I would have staged these plays if I were doing a full production? Probably not. And yet there was an extraordinary freedom in shrugging off the weight of past productions (and my own preconceptions) and simply serving the film as a whole; in asking the question—what role does this moment need to play in the film? What purpose does it serve? The first play that we did was *A Midsummer Night's Dream*, the final moment of Puck's

epilogue. When we rehearsed it, Luke Taylor (playing Puck) simply walked forward and spoke the lines of the speech standing centre stage, looking at Queen Elizabeth. When Roland saw what we had rehearsed, he was a little nonplussed.

"Couldn't he be more Puck-like?" he asked.

Of course! How I might direct that moment anywhere else was irrelevant. At this moment in the film, we needed to see Young Oxford full of life, spirited—Puck-like. And

107

the camera needed to see him ducking in and out of the painted trees, creating different pictures and new angles.

And so it was with each play. And with the journey of the plays as a whole—from the overtly theatrical and over-the-top Jonson play at the beginning of the film through to the absolute stillness and psychological complexity of Hamlet's "To be or not to be."

And somewhere in the middle was the day when everything came together and something magical happened. It was the day of the press junket when lots of journalists were descending on Babelsberg and visiting the set in groups throughout the day. And we had, I don't know, five hundred extras, maybe more. And we only had Mark Rylance with us for a day because of his theatre commitments in London. So we had to get it all done. It should have been the most stressful day imaginable. But instead, something magical happened. The theatre held us captive. And we held our breath as first Mark and then Alex Hassell (playing Spencer) spoke words of such power and beauty, with such skill and truth that everyone just listened. And a theatre full of German extras, many of whom couldn't understand the words, understood—somehow—the tale that was being told. And when King Henry reached out his hand to them, to his band of brothers, they reached back. And just for a moment, it was four hundred years ago, we were hearing the words of Henry V's Crispin Day speech for the very first time and we would have followed our King into any battle. And then Roland said, "Cut," and the world moved on. ❀

EVERY MAN OUT OF HIS HUMOUR
by Ben Jonson

"I've just read the whole play," Alex Hassell said when he called me a couple of weeks before filming began, "Is it possible that it's really not very good?"

And he's not wrong. It's a play that hasn't really stood the test of time—full of contemporary references and humor that may have been hysterical four hundred years ago but has since been utterly lost in the mists of time. In our film, however, it needed to serve only two purposes— to introduce us to the colorful, life-filled, vibrant world of the Rose theatre and to give Oxford a glimpse of how a word or action in a play might influence thousands of people in one moment. So we stuck two actors up a tree in comedy red shoes, persuaded James Garnon to do his impression of a horse, got the groundlings laughing and talking and jostling each other a-plenty and dressed Alex in a costume designed to mimic and mock the lord sitting above him in the gentleman's box. Not a great play but a great storytelling device. —TH

HENRY V

Have we shot our bolt? In wanting to make the Rose seem completely magical when Oxford first sees it, have we left ourselves nowhere to go when we need the entire theatre to be bewitched by the brilliance of *Henry V* (the first of Oxford's plays to be performed—anonymously—at the Rose)? . . . Luckily, sometimes things just work out. And so, with great good fortune, one of the greatest Shakespearean actors of our time, Mark Rylance, agrees to come and play the Chorus and thus speak the first of Oxford's words to be heard in a public playhouse. And when he tells us that it is our imaginations that will fill this theatre with princes and kings, with the proud hooves of horses and with battalions of men, we believe him. And when Alex Hassell, utterly compelling as Henry himself, tells us that we who fight with him shall be remembered from this day to the ending of the world, of course men and women in the crowd jump up on stage to battle the French. And when Rhys Ifans, as Oxford, watching from the Lords Rooms, leaps to his feet, draws his sword and cries, "Death to the French!" it is both hysterically funny and completely perfect all at the same time. —TH

ROMEO AND JULIET

In Act I, scene V of *Romeo and Juliet*, Romeo sees Juliet for the first time and falls instantly, truly, madly, fatally in love with her. In the film, Oxford watches this scene on the stage of the Rose and we follow his mind back in time to the moment when he, newly married but still in love with Elizabeth, beheld her once more in a dance at court and began the affair that would eventually lead to his downfall. The words in the play tell us of Juliet's breathtaking beauty and of the overwhelming immediacy of Romeo's love—and therefore by extension all that Oxford is feeling—but it is Lisy Christl's exquisite costumes (the arresting, flame-orange dress of Juliet) and Claire van Kampen's intricate musical arrangements (of the beautiful *Branle de la Torche*) that truly link the two moments in time. —TH

Did my heart love till now?
Forswear it sight,
For I ne'er saw true beauty
till this night

Double, double, toil and trouble.

MONTAGE OF JULIUS CAESAR, MACBETH, *AND* TWELFTH NIGHT

The challenge: to find three brief moments from three of the plays that are recognizable to the film's audience as ever-enduring classic drama (be it comedy or tragedy or something else entirely) but are also, somehow, unclichéd—allowing us to appreciate the breadth and still-surprising nature of the plays. . . Easy job then . . . Of course, in the end, all you can do is stage each moment as simply and truthfully as possible and try and rest secure in the knowledge that four hundred years ago these moments wouldn't have been clichés: the sorcery of *Macbeth*'s witches ("Double, double, toil and trouble. . .") performed during an age of vicious witch-hunts would have sent shivers down the spine of every Elizabethan and the brutal murder of Caesar would have had the gripping intensity of a particularly gruesome thriller. And then there's *Twelfth Night*—probably the least known of the three but able to tick the right boxes—a meeting of twins (that classic Shakespearean device), a brilliant moment of situational rather than farcical comedy (when Olivia discovers that there's an identical version of the man she loves, she simply exclaims, "Most wonderful!") and, perhaps more truthfully the reason I wanted it in, one of my favorite moments in all of Shakespeare and a private homage to Tim Carroll, the man who taught me pretty much everything I know about the plays by the man we call William Shakespeare. —TH

HAMLET "To be, or not to be"

A man sits alone on a stage. Is it better, he asks the audience before him, to suffer all the heartache and the pain that the world throws at us or to end it all by taking one's own life, thus risking an eternity of suffering? In the court, Queen Elizabeth, lonely in her old age, sits silently bewitched by the power of Oxford's words. In the Rose Theatre, hundreds of groundlings stand, captivated, oblivious to the rain that drenches them as they listen. Which they actually did with very good grace, even when one of the roof coverings used to control the light started catching the rain, billowing in the breeze and then dumping huge sheets of water on the unsuspecting extras below. Still they held their place; still they looked on in silent wonder. Though, to be fair, that may have had more to do with a terror of ruining the take rather than a complete absorption in "To be, or not to be" . . . perhaps ours is not to reason why. —TH

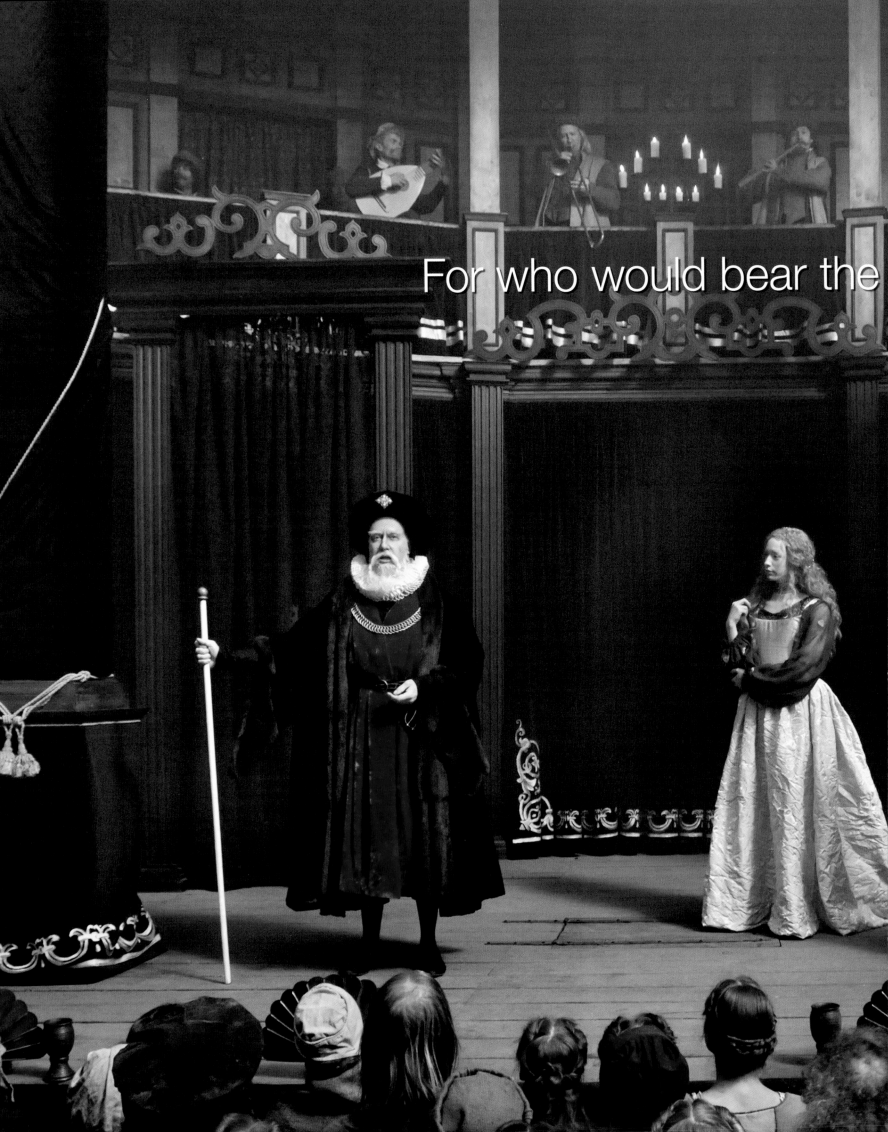

For who would bear the

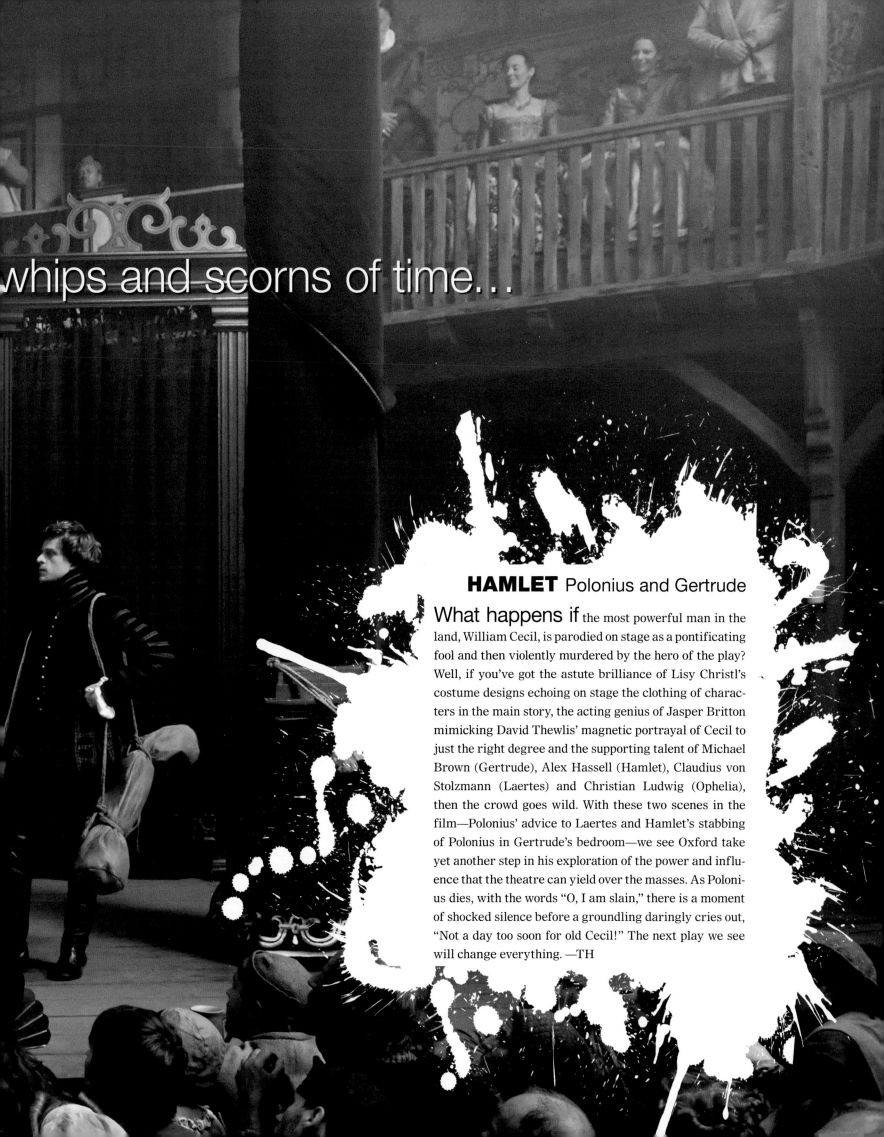

...whips and scorns of time...

HAMLET Polonius and Gertrude

What happens if the most powerful man in the land, William Cecil, is parodied on stage as a pontificating fool and then violently murdered by the hero of the play? Well, if you've got the astute brilliance of Lisy Christl's costume designs echoing on stage the clothing of characters in the main story, the acting genius of Jasper Britton mimicking David Thewlis' magnetic portrayal of Cecil to just the right degree and the supporting talent of Michael Brown (Gertrude), Alex Hassell (Hamlet), Claudius von Stolzmann (Laertes) and Christian Ludwig (Ophelia), then the crowd goes wild. With these two scenes in the film—Polonius' advice to Laertes and Hamlet's stabbing of Polonius in Gertrude's bedroom—we see Oxford take yet another step in his exploration of the power and influence that the theatre can yield over the masses. As Polonius dies, with the words "O, I am slain," there is a moment of shocked silence before a groundling daringly cries out, "Not a day too soon for old Cecil!" The next play we see will change everything. —TH

RICHARD III

Historically, it is the play *Richard II* that is linked to the Essex rebellion. However, without the benefit of a lengthy footnote (see page 98), this is fairly tricky to convey to an audience that doesn't consist entirely of Shakespeare scholars. And so instead it is *Richard III* that we use in the film to incite the groundlings to rebellion and revolt. Funnily enough, although in many ways this scene is the climax towards which all the plays have been building, the filming of it in my memory is less about the play itself and more about watching the wonderful Mark Rylance getting pelted with fruit and vegetables over and over and over again. —TH

Things growing, are not ripe

ACT V
BEHIND THE SCENES

WE ARE SUCH STUFF AS DREAMS ARE MADE ON

Over sixty-three days the cast of *Anonymous*, which included fifty-nine speaking roles, 8,400 extras, and twenty-nine animals (mostly horses) assembled, rehearsed, emoted, and suffered their way through hair and make-up, sometimes 750 in one day; none enduring more than David Thewlis who played William Cecil over a forty-year period.

On seventy-four sets, built and managed by nearly 400 people at Studio Babelsberg in Potsdam, Germany (and 1 day at Hebbel Theatre in Berlin), they also danced, watched plays, dueled, plotted, revolted, and chopped off heads.

But before shooting could begin, months were spent designing cities and dresses and renaissance theatres— and even 20,000 virtual extras.

Extras at Studio Babelsberg getting costumes (lower right), hair and make-up (left), and lunch (top).

Ruffs, Cuffs & FARTHINGALES

Lisy Christl
Costume Designer

Irst of all I read the script, and met the director, Roland Emmerich, because I needed to know if he already had ideas I would have to incorporate into an existing concept or if the canvas was blank. Next I tried to read as much as possible about the era to learn about the politics and culture of that time—as well as their dress—because I wanted to know what the world looked like in the sixteenth century. I wanted to know what they believed, thought and worried about. I wanted to understand the era.

Then, working closely with an historian and studying paintings of the sixteenth and seventeenth centuries, I developed an historic and atmospheric documentation. And because the main characters of our movie were celebrities there were numerous portraits available that were extremely helpful. I broke the clothes in the portraits into

Anonymous

categories like cuts, accessories, jewelry, fabric, colors, underwear, and shoes, and I considered well-known preferences like the expensive tastes of Queen Elizabeth I. Then I covered the walls of my studio with photos and conceptual designs and it just so happened that a small picture of Karl Lagerfeld was hanging below a portrait of the Earl of Oxford. Roland saw it and asked me why it was hanging there. I said, "Because to me, Karl Lagerfeld is a modern Earl of Oxford with his tight, high collars." And that was *exactly* what Roland had been thinking for weeks. Luckily, we were on the same wavelength.

For the women we stayed close to the historical paintings. But the men we decided to put in high boots and pants with softer cuts because the historical cuts looked like short balloon skirts and, with their skinny legs and clumsy shoes sticking out, they looked bizarre. Costumes need to match the characters and our noblemen could not look ridiculous.

Southampton stood out, however. He was the only nobleman at the English Court who still had long hair. His long, curly hair was so prominent and striking that it allowed us to approach and deal with his costumes more freely. For him we found Rumanian costume aprons with a beautiful golden and silver embroidery that had exactly the same opulence and depth of the embroidery of the sixteenth century and, therefore, looked absolutely authentic. The fabric matched his character—a wealthy Earl—and the camera loved it.

Elizabeth, naturally was a major undertaking. We saw the younger Elizabeth as approachable so her skirts were softer, the colors were soft green, orange, and red to

Knogen
□ *gold*

black. In England during the sixteenth century, colors as well as materials for the different classes were regulated by law. For example, silk and the colors black, red, and green were exclusively reserved for nobility.

The portraits of older Elizabeth, however, clearly show her intention to demonstrate great power through her clothes. The thought, "power through fashion," stuck in my head so her cuts changed to stiff farthingales and other typical sixteenth-century skirts. Her dresses became more sumptuous, the collars higher, and her hair decoration became more sweeping and protruding.

Around the third time I met with Roland we had patterns of cloth and work samples for almost all the characters. And so we started quite a pragmatic process: "Yes, I like it. No, I don't like it," or "I want a different color." And shortly thereafter we set up workshops in three locations, two in the U.K. (at Sands Film and Cosprop) and one in Berlin. They became a kind of haute couture laboratory for sixteenth-century clothes. There was a wardrobe mistress, who drew all the cuts and was in charge of fittings, and we had wonderful dressmakers whose knowledge and skills were a great gift. We also had a milliner, a jeweler, a collar maker, a separate dyeing and aging workshop and much more.

Our workshop motto was "Let's try this now." So we would throw fabric into washing machines, wash and dye it and afterward we would gather around and examine the result. Having so many enthusiastic people sharing a great passion for old fabric, paintings, and costumes, and being able to have a go at everything right away—

ABOVE: *Lisy Christl (right) fitting an extra.*

131

abric ✓

tment same F. ✓

uie

er
au]

Suit

Cloak

from the idea of the fabric to the color—was fantastic and an incredibly creative way to work. This is what makes *Anonymous* so different from all the other movies I've worked on. This "laboratory" offered me great freedom and stimulated everyone involved in the creative process.

Beside our main actors I had to dress approximately 1,500 other people. That included the three main groups of extras: "nobility," "bourgeoisie," and "crowd," and then a third category: the theatre actors—the play-within-a-play characters—which was another substantial task.

In the end I felt it wasn't necessary to make strictly authentic copies of any of the clothes—we weren't making a documentary on the sixteenth-century English Court. That said, we never veered too far from the historical examples. And that's what I like most about my work, creating a playful transformation of the genuine article. The longer I concentrate on an era, the less restricted I feel. And from that comes the most wonderful things.

After the screening of the first rough cut with Roland he told me the characters looked as if they had chosen their dresses themselves that morning. That was simply the greatest compliment that I could have gotten, because, in the end, it is all about empathy that we, the audience, feel for the characters. And that's what makes movie magic. ❧

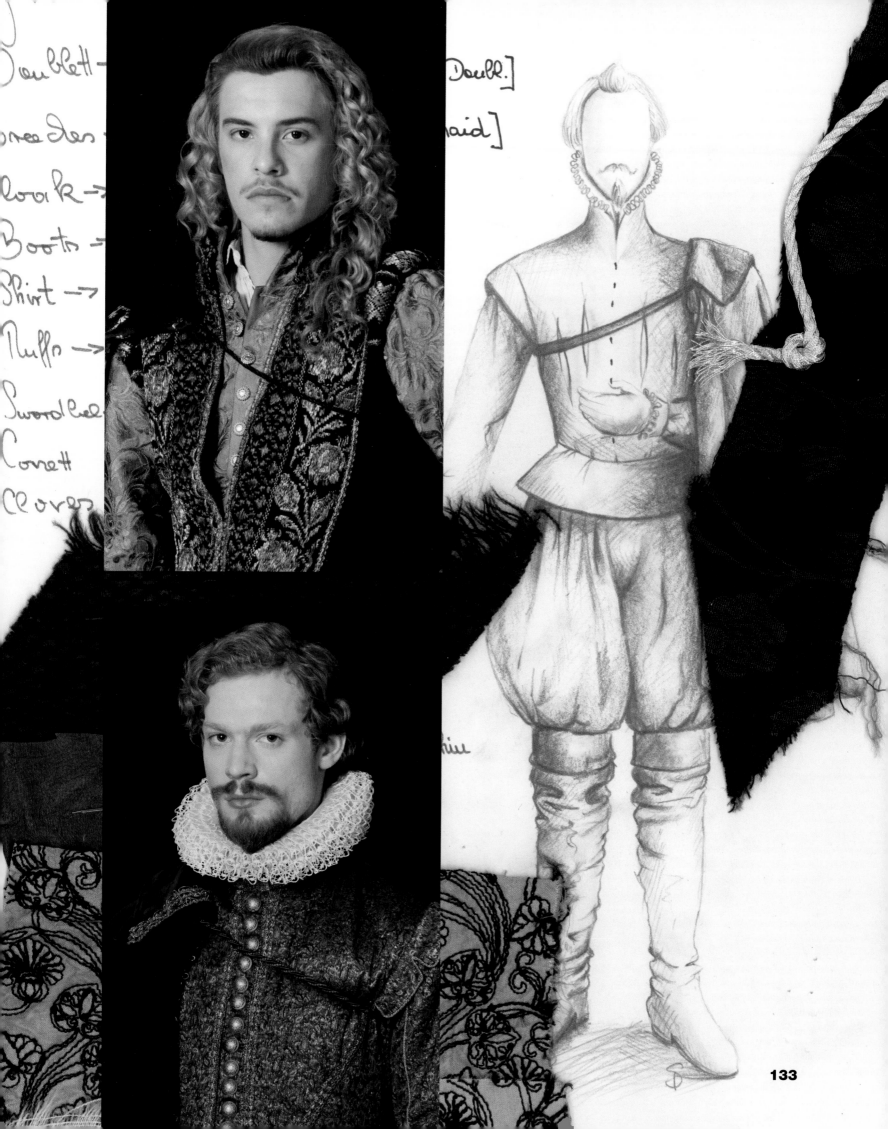

Doublett—
breedes
Cloak →
Boots →
Shirt →
Ruffs →
Sword belt
Corsett
Gloves

[Doubl.]
[maid]

The Rose,
BY ANY OTHER NAME

Sebastian Krawinkel
Production Designer

Roland's idea was to shoot plates in real locations to use later as backgrounds for scenes shot on the green screen stage. So in September 2009 Roland, the DP Anna Foerster, producer Robert Leger, line producer Arno Neubauer, location manager Giles Edleston, and I spent a week touring England looking at mansions as well as Dover Castle, the Tower of London, and other beautiful places. It was like driving right into the sixteenth century and the details, colors and finishes we discovered really helped in designing the sets. Next I bought every book available about Elizabethan England and its architecture and, of course, I traveled extensively on the Internet! Then I pinned all my research up on the walls of my office and dug in.

The Globe and the Rose theatres were fairly demanding because only their foundations still exist. There are no references of the interiors, and exterior illustrations from the sixteenth century are not reliable because each one looks different. I looked at the rebuilt Globe in London, of course, but didn't stick to its original size. I shrunk it to fit my budget and, in the end, used one set for both theatres. The Rose I gave a rural feel like a wooden barn, dark and dramatic in color and aged about twenty years, whereas the Globe is brand-new with cut-glass stones that sparkle in the light referencing the influence of the queen's palaces and her bejeweled fashion sense.

LEFT: *Sebastian Krawinkel (left) with Roland Emmerich on the Globe set.* OPPOSITE: *Concept illustrations for the Rose (top), and the Globe (bottom) sets.*

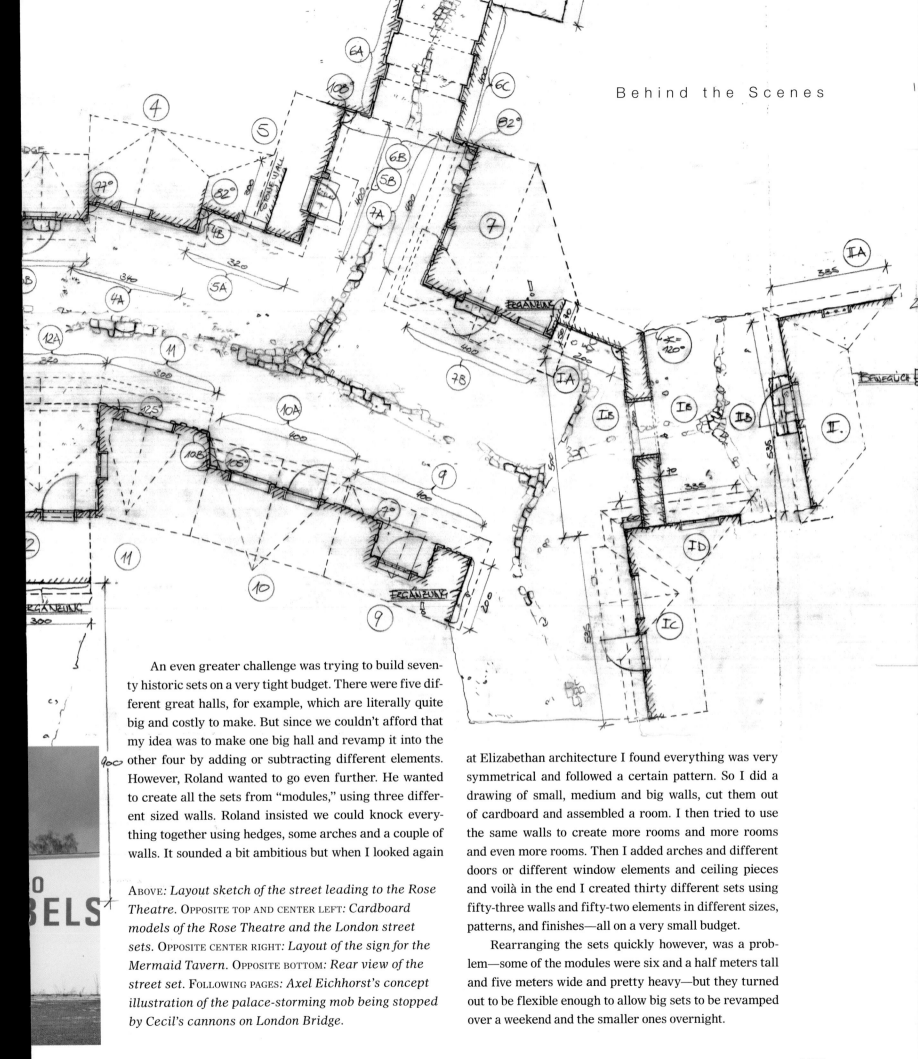

An even greater challenge was trying to build seventy historic sets on a very tight budget. There were five different great halls, for example, which are literally quite big and costly to make. But since we couldn't afford that my idea was to make one big hall and revamp it into the other four by adding or subtracting different elements. However, Roland wanted to go even further. He wanted to create all the sets from "modules," using three different sized walls. Roland insisted we could knock everything together using hedges, some arches and a couple of walls. It sounded a bit ambitious but when I looked again

at Elizabethan architecture I found everything was very symmetrical and followed a certain pattern. So I did a drawing of small, medium and big walls, cut them out of cardboard and assembled a room. I then tried to use the same walls to create more rooms and more rooms and even more rooms. Then I added arches and different doors or different window elements and ceiling pieces and voilà in the end I created thirty different sets using fifty-three walls and fifty-two elements in different sizes, patterns, and finishes—all on a very small budget.

Rearranging the sets quickly however, was a problem—some of the modules were six and a half meters tall and five meters wide and pretty heavy—but they turned out to be flexible enough to allow big sets to be revamped over a weekend and the smaller ones overnight.

ABOVE: *Layout sketch of the street leading to the Rose Theatre.* OPPOSITE TOP AND CENTER LEFT: *Cardboard models of the Rose Theatre and the London street sets.* OPPOSITE CENTER RIGHT: *Layout of the sign for the Mermaid Tavern.* OPPOSITE BOTTOM: *Rear view of the street set.* FOLLOWING PAGES: *Axel Eichhorst's concept illustration of the palace-storming mob being stopped by Cecil's cannons on London Bridge.*

A-A   ELEVATION 9   GANGBAR   ELEVATION 10A   ELEVATION 10B

ABOVE: *Drawing of houses along the street leading to the Rose Theatre by Stephan Speth.* BELOW: *The finished set.*

But the most daunting task on this film—above and beyond designing all the sets—was designing the virtual world. There were great halls and theatres for the actors to play on, yes, but then we also needed to design all of sixteenth-century London. Roland wanted to show the geographic relationships between, let's say, the Tower and the Bridge or Oxford's house. He wanted to let the audience know where they were.

ABOVE AND OPPOSITE: *Concept illustrations by Axel Eichhorst of London Bridge and the Tower of London showing Oxford waiting for Southampton.*

So we started with historic maps and from there designed the major elements like London Bridge, the Tower and St. Paul's. Some elements like the Tower and St. Paul's were easy because there are plenty of drawings and models from that time to look at, and in fact, most of the Tower is still standing. Other things, like London Bridge and Whitehall Palace, however, presented more of a challenge.

My goal was to draw the whole world in 3D supplying files good enough so that Marc Weigert and Volker Engel (the VFX Department) could bring them to life. But first we put Roland in front of the computer so he could choose

143

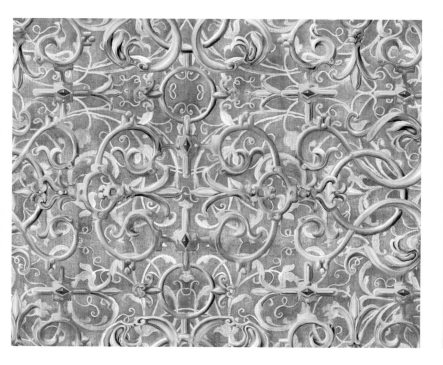

OPPOSITE TOP: *Filming Elizabeth and Oxford's first meeting in the kitchen set of Hedingham Castle.* OPPOSITE BOTTOM LEFT: *Backdrop painting for* Every Man Out of His Humour *by Ilona Velvela.* OPPOSITE BELOW RIGHT: *Theatre set models.* ABOVE: *Ornamental wall paneling detail used on the Globe Theatre set.* ABOVE RIGHT: *Oxford's prison cell set in the Tower.* BELOW: *Detail of wallpaper designed by Axel Eichhorst for the Queen's room at Hampton Court.*

all the different angles for his shots and from there we would know which designs needed special attention and what we would see in the background. We gave the VFX department ideas for textures and finishes and they generated the city model that we see in the movie. Wide shots, like the helicopter shots of London, are rarely seen in movies about that period but Marc and Volker did it and it makes the movie a unique experience. It is fantastic!

It is a huge collaboration and I am very pleased at how everything turned out. The printed "Gobelin" tapestries, the small stone modules made of Styrofoam and covered with flexible paint in the torture chamber, and Oxford's prison cell (where plaster would have been too heavy) all turned out amazing.

All I can do is thank my fantastic team—not only the whole art department filled with skilled draftsmen, art directors and expert computer illustrators—but also the craftsmen from Studio Babelsberg—they are why this came together and worked so well.

Walking onto a dressed set with the actors on it and the right light and atmosphere is always the best and most enjoyable moment for me, of course only if the director is happy and loves the set! But it lasts just until the first scene is shot. After that the set usually gets torn to pieces; walls will be taken out and everything is filled up with gear and coffee cups. So the moment between a beautifully dressed and finished set and total chaos is normally very short. But then, it lives on in the cinema. ❀

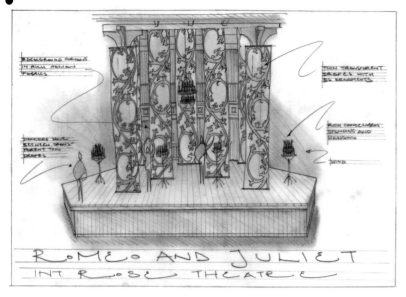

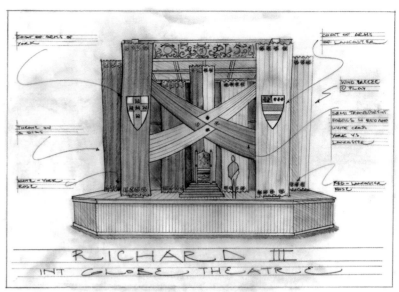

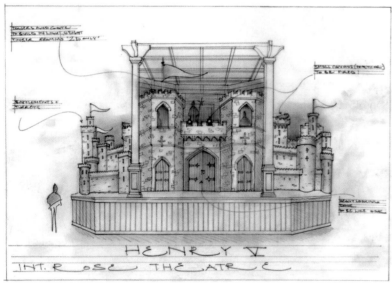

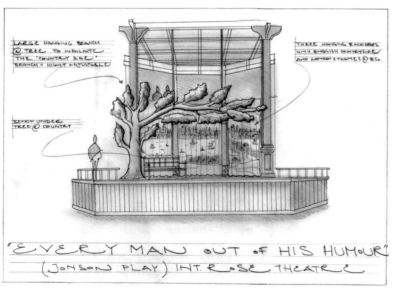

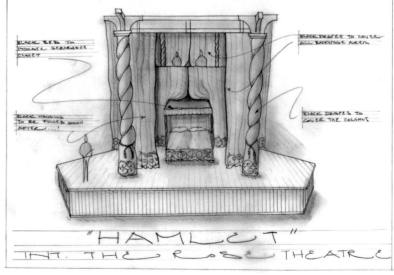

ABOVE: *Design sketches by Sebastian Krawinkel for various theatre sets.* OPPOSITE: *Mark Rylance playing the humpbacked Gloucester in* Richard III.

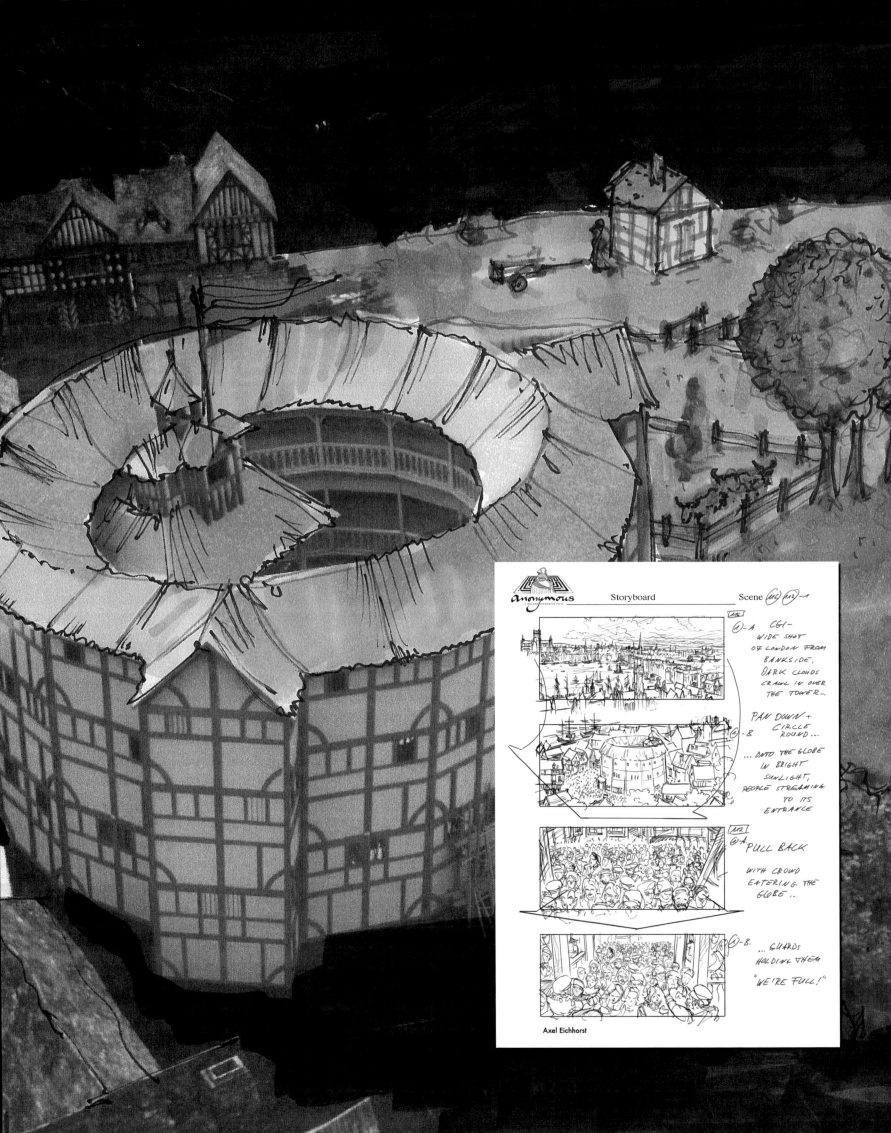

Axel Eichhorst

If This Be Magic,
LET IT BE AN ART

Volker Engel & Marc Weigert
Visual Effects Supervisors

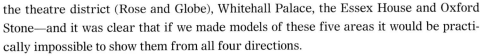

A movie about Shakespeare doesn't necessarily bring visual effects to mind. But after speaking with Roland about the project we knew that, at the very least, we would have to reproduce the entire city of London.

Our first step was to decide between miniature models or 3D computer models. Roland wanted to have wide shots primarily of five different parts of the city—the Tower, the theatre district (Rose and Globe), Whitehall Palace, the Essex House and Oxford Stone—and it was clear that if we made models of these five areas it would be practically impossible to show them from all four directions.

Plus with a real model, what you shoot that day is what you get, whereas a computer model is flexible. Perspectives can be changed later and you can see whether a shot works within the context of a live action scene and improve it if you want. Furthermore, there are an incredible amount of moving details that you would need to add separately

OPPOSITE: *Color sketch of the Globe Theatre and its surroundings by Sebastian Krawinkel and storyboard of the crowd arriving at the Globe by Axel Eichhorst.*
ABOVE TOP: *Visual Effects Supervisors and Executive Producers Volker Engel (left) and Marc Weigert (right).* ABOVE: *Final frame from the Globe flyover scene.*

149

anyway: people, animals, or ships with moving sails, let's say. So we went with computer rendering.

Our goal was to recreate the city as accurately as possible. We started with two very detailed maps of old London that had every street and alley marked, then we measured everything and divided the city into sections. Next we placed all the large roads in our digital replica of the city, only very rarely making use of artistic freedom to deviate a little from the map.

But because London burned down several times over the centuries there is no area left to shoot Elizabethan-era backgrounds. However, outside London we found fantastic buildings that still exist from that time, so we took a photo tour through England to gather images for our virtual world.

Many of the houses we found were crooked and we thought they had become that way over time. But it turns out that they were built crooked, so they exist today pretty much in their original state. We took photos of approximately 500 to 600 buildings from all sides, even using a photo tower (a remote-controlled telescopic system that extended fifteen meters), enabling us to photograph very old thatched and slate roofs.

Then we used these images to texture our virtual buildings by applying a photographic wallpaper of bricks, roof tiles or thatch, for example. And thus, step by step, we put together the houses to form the streets, and finally the entire city.

ABOVE: *The raw CG light pass for the Tower of London shot shown opposite top.* OPPOSITE TOP: *From a busy marketplace on the left to William Cecil's carriage in the center, hundreds of details make this computer-generated Tower of London shot come to life.* OPPOSITE LEFT: *A mixture of sun and clouds give the street leading to the Essex house a menacing feel.* OPPOSITE BOTTOM RIGHT: *While the crowd and London Bridge are completely computer generated the river consists of real-water elements composited into the image.*

ABOVE: *The thirty-second long shot of Queen Elizabeth's funeral procession is the longest entirely computer-generated shot in* Anonymous. BELOW: *Anne de Vere in the Oxford Stone studio set-up (top) and the finished shot (bottom).* OPPOSITE TOP: *Computer-generated scene of Essex walking to his execution in the Tower of London courtyard.* OPPOSITE BELOW: *Essex and Southampton in the Whitehall Palace studio set-up (top) and the composited shot (bottom).*

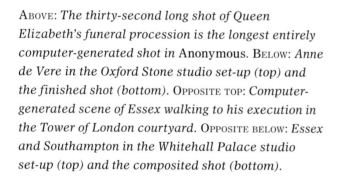

Then we could use our virtual London for specific shots. One very complex shot is Queen Elizabeth's funeral procession on the frozen Thames. Normally a shot lasts five to seven seconds, but this one is over thirty. It is a helicopter flight over London Bridge where tens of thousands of spectators are on their way to the funeral procession. To the left and right we see parts of the city and docked sailing ships with collapsed ice around them. This is one of the few shots we actually started preparing on the very first day—and didn't finish until about ten months later.

To build this shot, we started with the London background already created (the bridge, the buildings, the river), then made digital people (one by one) by virtually building a skeleton and giving each figure an animation (walk through the shot or pick something up), added clothes (fabric movement created by the computer must be done even for tiny figures, because you immediately recognize if that's missing or done inaccurately), and repeated until we had all our extras.

In the end, you have dozens of elements—houses, roads, ships, people—which must be assembled into a scene. When this is done, the entire scene assembly has to be lit; this is called CG Lighting. Then it must be rendered by dozens of machines in many different "passes," like the "reflection pass," which deals with all reflections (on windows for example), and the "shadow pass," which

152

deals with only shadows of objects, and many others.

Finally, we go to compositing where all passes and all the real elements—the live actors that have been shot on the green screens—are put together. Changes are made as needed to lighting, and fog, clouds, and chimney smoke are added. And that's why a shot like the funeral scene can take ten months from the very first concept to its completion.

We worked on a total of 354 shots—only 311 of which ended up in the film—with a crew of thirty-five artists, technicians, and production personnel. We used about seventy-five computers, all with dual quad-core processors. So seventy-five times eight equals 600 render cores, most with twenty-four gigabytes of RAM. We needed some with forty-eight gigs to render the really big shots, and yet we still had to divide those shots into parts. The funeral procession, for example, had more than 20,000 digital extras whose digital clothing had to move naturally in the wind. One single computer cannot create that, so the scene was divided into several parts and then reassembled later. On average, we have about twenty-five different passes per render. When you calculate this for the large shots that are split into six or seven different parts, it means six times twenty-five different passes per frame multiplied by 100 to 120 frames. The disc space requirements for the whole project were about sixty terabytes, or about sixty million megabytes. Backing up took two weeks.

The most important thing is to always keep in mind what the shot is all about. Every shot is telling a story and that's why we give a lot of thought to things like the light mood, what's in shadow, what's in the light, where the fog should be placed and how dense it should be.

And screenings for *Anonymous* are important, too, since, on this project, we are not only visual effects supervisors but executive producers. ❈

Betrayal Is
BORN IN DARKNESS

Anna J. Foerster
Director of Photography

When Roland Emmerich and I first started talking about the look for *Anony-mous*, it became immediately clear that the film needed to feel very different from a typical period film where sunlit rooms, romantic candlelight, and cozy fires in the kitchen set the tone. We wanted *Anonymous* to be somber and dark following the idea that conspiracies and betrayal are born in darkness, and that some characters live best in the shadows.

Just as we started preparing for *Anonymous* digital cameras reached a new level. And despite the fact that I had never shot digitally and that a period film doesn't necessarily lend itself to digital cinematography, we decided to embrace the new technology because it allowed us to use candles as light sources, giving us a new, exciting storytelling tool.

While scouting in England I became fascinated with the light that came through the old glass windows. The uneven surfaces, air bubbles, and even color differentiation found among the panes gave it a very particular feel that I wanted to replicate. And, although we couldn't use real glass, due to weight and cost, we found the right mix by testing many different materials and adjusting the warping, air bubbles, and sandblasting. Vermeer was my inspiration for the kind of muted daylight I wanted to recreate on stage. But I also wanted to slightly distort and diffuse the view looking out, too, so we could use painted backgrounds relatively close to our sets. In the end our windows acted as a kind of mini-motif. Many scenes take place in front of these glass frames making the characters seem almost

ABOVE: Director of Photography Anna J. Foerster and Roland Emmerich

155

trapped, peering at the world outside, which, because of social position and circumstance, they are not a part of.

Most days in our story are gloomy, dark, and often on the brink of dusk or dawn, so sunlight is used sparingly and only for scenes where it emotionally contributes to the story, like the first time we enter the theatre, or when young Oxford—the golden child—arrives at his new home bringing light into the dark rooms of the Cecil house. And at first the Queen is surrounded by radiant light which seems to come from within her. But during the course of the story the glow becomes extinguished as she is forced to step into the harsh daylight that is invading her world.

Because there was nothing but firelight and candles to light dark places in Elizabethan times, I wanted to light rooms and faces without using modern sources. Fluorescence may be something we're used to today but on a subconscious level the audience would feel that there is something inauthentic about that light in a period film, so candles play an enormous roll in all of our sets.

The painter George de la Tour had an incredibly dramatic way of using a single candle to light a scene with the glow extending far into the background. I kept his technique in mind while lighting rooms that should appear to be only lit by a few candles or a single fireplace by adding candles and modern lights outside the frame or carefully hiding them within the frame. For even more light we had double and triple wick candles made which burn much brighter and have a nice, lively flame. Plays at court during Elizabethan times were lit with lard candles, which—aside from giving off a revolting smell—created a thin veil of soot giving the actors a unique, almost romantic aura. So we used lots of atmospheric smoke to acquire that diffused and soft luminosity.

Most of our scenes in old London were shot on a large green screen stage with the backgrounds and set extensions created digitally. I referenced some Turner paintings for light and mood to design the light for these scenes. It is very important to understand the lighting of the entire image even when you only shoot a small part of it in front of a green screen. Then, together with the VFX team, angles and distances need to be precisely calculated and often put into storyboards to achieve a seamless transition between what is shot on stage and what gets added later.

We also used lighting, choice of lenses, and camera movement to underscore the emotional context of a scene. For example, we used wide angle lenses and very little movement at court during performances to highlight the idea that the nobility is constrained by their corsets and social graces. And when the young Elizabeth and young Oxford are first in love we used greater movement and longer lenses because the narrower depth of field isolates the couple from the background, emotionally removing them from their surroundings. But as the story evolves, the lenses become wider, the depths of the rooms grow sharper and their surroundings seem to confine them.

The visual journey into Elizabethan times was definitely a learning experience. I now know exactly how many candles were used to light a Shakespeare play and how they, too, used light to create drama. Plays were timed precisely so act one happened during daylight, act two at twilight and act three by candle light controlled with a sophisticated system to dim on cue. All of this was my inspiration. For me, however, it is not about being historically accurate or simply creating beautiful images. My desire is that every shot, every light situation evokes an emotion that serves the story. ❀

What's in a name? That which we call a ros

EPILOGUE
by any other name would smell as sweet

EXT. THE ROSE THEATRE– DAWN

Jonson's eyes search the ground. And, eventually, he finds it— The metal box that seems to somehow have survived the conflagration.

Jonson opens the box. Inside the box are the manuscripts Oxford gave him. Jonson smiles, relieved. They are singed at the edges, but they are there. We hear—

> **PROLOGUE** *(O.S.)*
> O— for a muse of fire. . . that would ascend the brightest heaven of invention. . .
> A kingdom for a stage, princes to act, and monarchs to behold the swelling scene!

INT. BROADWAY THEATRE– STAGE–DUSK

"Prologue" turns and addresses his audience (and us) in the modern theatre.

> **PROLOGUE**
> Robert Cecil remained the most powerful man in the Court of King James, though he could not prevent the public theatres from becoming ever more popular. William Shakespeare, however, spent the remaining years of his life not in the playhouses of London, but in the small town of his birth, Stratford upon Avon, as a businessman and grain merchant. *(beat)*
> Ben Jonson succeeded in his desire to be the most celebrated playwright of his time, becoming England's first Poet Laureate. And in 1623, he wrote the dedication to the collected works of the man we call William Shakespeare. *(beat)* And so. . . though our story is finished, our poet's is not. For his monument is ever-living, made not of stone but of verse, and it shall be remembered. . . as long as words are made of breath and breath of life.

The curtains close.

FADE OUT.

Shakespeare's Body of Work

List of Shakespeare's Plays in Chronological Order

The Comedy of Errors
The Second Part of Henry VI
The Third Part of Henry VI
The First Part of Henry VI
Richard III
Titus Andronicus
The Taming of the Shrew
The Two Gentlemen of Verona
Loves Labor's Lost
Romeo & Juliet
Richard II
A Midsummer Night's Dream
King John
The Merchant of Venice
The First Part of Henry IV
The Second Part of Henry IV
Much Ado About Nothing

Henry V
Julius Caesar
As You Like It
Twelfth Night
Hamlet
The Merry Wives of Windsor
Troilus & Cressida
All's Well That Ends Well
Othello
Measure for Measure
Timon of Athens
King Lear
Macbeth
Antony & Cleopatra
Coriolanus
Pericles
Cymbeline

The Winter's Tale
The Tempest
Henry VIII
The Two Noble Kinsmen

The Poems
Venus & Adonis
The Rape of Lucrece
The Sonnets
The Phoenix and the Turtle

Conjectured chronological listing from
The Complete Signet Classic Shakespeare,
Sylvan Barnet, General Editor ©1963 by
Sylvan Barnet, published by Harcourt
Brace Jovanovich, Inc., New York

Further Reading

Alias Shakespeare by Joseph Sobran (Free Press, 1997)

The Anglican Shakespeare by Daniel L. Wright (Pacific-Columbia Books, 1994)

Burbage and Shakespeare's Stage by Charlotte C. Stopes (Haskell, 1970)

The Case for Edward de Vere as William Shakespeare by Percy Allen (C. Palmer, 1930)

Chasing Shakespeares by Sarah Smith (Washington Square Press, 2004)

'Counterfeiting' Shakespeare by Brian Vickers (Cambridge University Press, 2009)

The Courtier by Baldassare Castigliano, translation by Thomas Hoby with an Introduction by Walter Raleigh (David Nutt, 1900)

The Crisis of the Aristocracy: 1558–1641 by Lawrence Stone (Oxford University Press, 1967)

De Vere as Shakespeare: An Oxfordian Reading of the Canon by William Farina (McFarland & Company, 2005)

The de Veres of Castle Hedingham by Verily Anderson (Terence Dalton, 1993)

Discovering Shakespeare: A Festschrift in Honour of Isabel Holden by Daniel Wright (Shakespeare Authorship Research Centre, 2009)

Edward de Vere A Great Elizabethan by George Frisbee (Kessinger Publishing, 2003)

Elizabethan Mystery Man by Charles W. Barrell (A. Gauthier, 1940)

The Elizabethan Stage by E. K. Chambers (Oxford University Press, 2009)

English Studies or Essays in English History and Literature by John Sherren Brewer (John Murray, 1881)

The First Elizabeth by Carolly Erickson (Summit, 1983)

The Great Lord Burghley: A Study in Elizabethan Statecraft by Martin Hume (Cornell University Library, 2009)

Great Oxford: Essays on the Life and Work of Edward de Vere, 17th Earl of Oxford edited by Richard Malim (Parapress, 2004)

Hidden Allusions in Shakespeare's Plays by Eva Lee Turner Clark (Associated Faculty Press, 1976)

The History of the Worthies of England by Thomas Fuller (Thomas Tegg, 1840)

Lord Oxford Was Shakespeare by Montagu W. Douglas (Rich & Cowan, 1934)

The Lost Chronicle of Edward de Vere by Andrew Field (Viking, 1990)

The Man Who Was Shakespeare by Eva Turner Clark (R. R. Smith, 1937)

The Man Who Was Shakespeare by Charlton Ogburn (EPM Publications, 1995)

The Marginalia of Edward de Vere's Geneva Bible by Roger A. Stritmatter (Oxenford Press, 2001)

Monstrous Adversary by Alan H. Nelson (Liverpool University Press, 2003)

The Monument: "Shake-Speares Sonnets" by Edward de Vere, 17th Earl of Oxford by Hank Wittemore (Meadow Geese Press, 2005)

Mr. William Shakespeares Comedies, Histories, and Tragedies: A Facsimile of the First Folio, 1623 edited by Doug Moston (Routledge, 1998)

The Mysterious William Shakespeare by Charlton Ogburn (EPM Publications, 1989)

Oxford Dictionary of National Biography (www.oxforddnb.com), (Oxford University Press, 2004)

The Oxford-Shakespeare Case Corroborated by Percy Allen (C. Palmer, 1931)

Oxford: Son of Queen Elizabeth I by Paul Streitz (Oxford Institute Press, 2008)

Oxford's Letters, The Letters of Edward de Vere, 17th Earl of Oxford edited by Stephanie Hopkins Hughes, read by Derek Jacobi (Absolute Audiobooks, 2006)

People and Their Contexts: A Chronology of the 16th Century World by Sally Mosher (Xlibris Corporation, 2002)

The Polarisation of Elizabethan Politics: The Political Career of Robert Devereux, 2nd Earl of Essex, 1585–1597 (Cambridge: CUP, 1999)

The Private Character of Queen Elizabeth by Frederick Carleton Chamberlin (Lane, 1921)

The Profession of Dramatists in Shakespeare's Time, 1590–1642 by Gerald Eades Bentley (Princeton University Press, 1971)

The Profession of Player in Shakespeare's Time, 1590–1642 by Gerald Eades Bentley (Princeton University Press, 1984)

The Real Shakespeare: Retrieving the Early Years 1564–1594 by Dr. Eric Sams (Yale University Press, 1997)

The Relevance of Robert Greene to the Oxfordian Thesis by Stephanie Hopkins Hughes (Self-published, 1997)

Robert Devereux: Earl of Essex by G. B. Harrison (Henry Holt, 1937)

The Second Cecil, The Rise to Power (1563–1604) of Sir Robert Cecil, later first Earl of Salisbury by P. M. Handover (Eyre & Spottiswoode, 1959)

The Seventeenth Earl of Oxford by Bernard M. Ward (John Murray, 1928)

Shakespeare and Italy by Ernesto Grillo (Haskell, 1973)

Shakespeare and the Tudor Rose by Elisabeth Sears (Meadow Geese Press, 2003)

"Shakespeare" by Another Name by Mark Anderson (Gotham Books, 2006)

Shakespeare, Co-Author by Brian Vickers (Oxford University Press, 2004)

The Shakespeare Controversy: An Analysis of the Authorship Theories by Warren Hope and Kim Holston (Mcfarland & Co Inc., 1992)

Shakespeare Identified by J. Thomas Looney (Cecil Palmer, 1920)

The Shakespeare Problem Restated by Sir George Greenwood (Bodley Head, 1908)

Shakespeare Revealed in Oxford's Letters by William Plumer Fowler (Peter E. Randall, 1986)

Shakespeare's Ghost by James Webster Sherwood (Opus Books, 2000)

Shakespeare's Lost Kingdom: The True History of Shakespeare and Elizabeth by Charles Beauclerk (Grove Press, 2011)

Shakespeare's Unorthodox Biography by Diana Price (Greenwood Press, 2000)

Shakespeare: The Evidence by Ian Wilson (St. Martin's Griffin, 1999)

Shakespeare through Oxford Glasses by Hurbert Henry Holland (C. Palmer, 1923)

Shakespeare: Who Was He? by Richard F. Whalen (Praeger, 2008)

The Shakespearian Playing Companies by Andrew Gurr (Clarendon, 1996)

The Sources of Shakespeare's Plays by Kenneth A. Muir (Routledge, 2005)

Surveillance, Militarism and Drama in the Elizabethan Era by Curtis C. Breight (Palgrave Macmillian, 1996)

Tudor Politics: A Critical Approach to Topical Meaning by David Bevington (Harvard University Press, 1968)

The Virgin Queen by Christopher Hibbert (Da Capo Press, 1992)

Who Wrote Shakespeare? by John Michell (Thames & Hudson, 1999)

Cast & Crew

Columbia Pictures Presents

In association with
Relativity Media
A Centropolis Entertainment Production

In association with Studio Babelsberg

A Roland Emmerich Film

ANONYMOUS

Rhys Ifans
Vanessa Redgrave
Joely Richardson
David Thewlis
Xavier Samuel
Sebastian Armesto
Rafe Spall
Edward Hogg
Sam Reid
Jamie Campbell Bower
Trystan Gravelle
Helen Baxendale
with Mark Rylance
and Derek Jacobi

Casting by Leo Davis Lissy Holm

Costume Designer Lisy Christl

Visual Effects Supervisors
Volker Engel Marc Weigert

Co-Producer Kirstin Winkler

Co-Producers
Charlie Woebcken Christoph Fisser
Henning Molfenter

Executive Producers
Volker Engel Marc Weigert John Orloff

Music by
Thomas Wander and Harald Kloser

Edited by Peter R. Adam

Production Designer
Sebastian Krawinkel

Director of Photography Anna J. Foerster

Produced by
Roland Emmerich Larry Franco Robert Léger

Written by
John Orloff

Directed by
Roland Emmerich

CAST

Earl of Oxford	Rhys Ifans
Queen Elizabeth I	Vanessa Redgrave
Ben Jonson	Sebastian Armesto
William Shakespeare	Rafe Spall
William Cecil	David Thewlis
Robert Cecil	Edward Hogg
Earl of Southampton	Xavier Samuel
Earl of Essex	Sam Reid
Young Earl of Oxford	Jamie Campbell Bower
Young Queen Elizabeth I	Joely Richardson
Francesco	Paolo De Vita
Christopher Marlowe	Trystan Gravelle
Thomas Dekker	Robert Emms
Thomas Nashe	Tony Way
Captain Richard Pole	Julian Bleach
Prologue	Derek Jacobi
Spencer	Alex Hassell
Heminge	James Garnon
Condell	Mark Rylance
Pope	Jasper Britton
Sly	Michael Brown
Interrogator	Ned Dennehy
Philip Henslowe	John Keogh
Richard Burbage	Lloyd Hutchinson
Bessie Vavasour	Vicky Krieps
Anne De Vere	Helen Baxendale
Bridget De Vere	Paula Schramm
Young Anne De Vere	Amy Kwolek
Boy Earl of Oxford	Luke Taylor
Boy Robert Cecil	Isaiah Michalsky
Boy Earl of Southampton	Timo Huber
Archbishop	Richard Durdan
Footman	Shaun Lawton
John De Vere	Detlef Bothe
King James I	James Clyde
Cecil's Spy Servant	Christian Sengewald
Monsieur Beaulieu	Jean-Loup Fourure
Buxom Lady	Viktoria Gabrysch
Essex General	Axel Sichrovsky
Ladies-in-Waiting	Katrin Pollitt
	Patricia Grove
Selling Maid	Laura Lo Zito
Groundling	Gode Benedix
Usher	Nic Romm
Bear Baiter	Henry Lloyd-Hughes
Oxford's Servant	Patrick Diemling
Oxford's Doctor	Patrick Heyn
Stage Manager (New York)	Nino Sandow
Dwarf / Puck	Craig Salisbury
Quince	Rainer Guldener
Bottom	Trystan Pütter
Titania	André Kaczmarczyk
Child Oberon	Jonas Hämmerle
Child Titania	Leonard Kinzinger
Pole's Commander	Mike Maas
Stage Players: Shakespeare Company	Christian Leonard
	Christian Banzhaf
	Victor Calero
	Martin Engler

Stage Players: Shakespeare Company (cont.)	Alfred Hartung
	Oliver Kube
	Christian Ludwig
	Oliver Rickenbacher
	Claudius Von Stolzmann
Theatre Scenes Staged by	Tamara Harvey
Line Producer	Marcus Loges
Unit Production Manager	Miki Emmrich
First Assistant Director	Christopher Doll
Second Assistant Director	Tanja Däberitz
Stunt Coordinator	Rainer Werner
Assistant Stunt Coordinator	Armin Sauer
Stunts	Steve Thiede
	Karsten Schmidt
	Thomas Jester
	Mathias Bark
	Katja Kerstin Köhler
	Jockel Neubauer
	Thorsten Pabst
	Zsolt Séra
	Uli Richter
	Matthias Guenther
	Laszlo Ujvari
	Mathias Hoffmann
	Moritz Prochnow
	Matthias Fach
	Levente Tamasi
	Daniel Bohn
	Mike Schramm
Horse Master	Sandor Czirjak
Supervising Art Director	Stephan Gessler
Art Directors	Stefan Speth
	Sabine Engelberg
	Bryce Tibbey
	Kim Fredericksen
Set Decorator	Simon Boucherie
Property Master	Michael Fechner
Script Supervisor	Gabriella Gobber
"A" Camera / Steadicam Operator	Sebastian Meuschel
"B" Camera Operator	Vladimir Subotic
"C" Camera Operator	Philip Peschlow
1st Assistant "A" Camera	Birgit Dierken
1st Assistant "B" Camera	Johnny Feurer
1st Assistant "C" Camera	Alexander Von Wasilewski
2nd Assistant "A" Camera	Carmen Hearne
2nd Assistant "B" Camera	Mira Hamza
Digital Intermediate Technicians	Timo Andert
	Eddie Handschak
QC Coordinator	Jeffrey Yaworski
Camera Trainee	Cristian Pirjol
Costume Supervisor	Brigitta Fink
Costume Design Assistant	Susanne Niedergall

Costume Coordinator . . . . Almut Stier
Head Aging, Dying,
Theatre Costumes . . . . Marie Heitzinger
Costumers . . . . Gregory Nelson
Petra Gärstke
Sonia Rocha
Natalia Riede
Daniela Backes
Dietke Brandt
Ramona Klinikowski
Martina Steiner
Costume Houses . . . . Sands Film
Cosprops
Angels The Costumiers

Key Hair . . . . Heike Merker
Key Makeup . . . . Björn Rehbein
Makeup / Hair Artists . . . . Daniela Skala
Sabine Schumann
Anna Evenkamp
Christiane Weber
Helmut Rühl
Julia Lechner

Gaffer . . . . Albrecht Silberberger
Best Boy Electric . . . . Roland Patzelt
Electricians . . . . Peter Kramer
Alexander Zeihn
Björn Koerner
Georg Simmendinger
Hinrich Peters
Rigging Gaffer . . . . Dietmar Haupt
Key Grip . . . . Dieter Bähr
Best Boy Grip . . . . Christian Scheibe
Dolly Grip . . . . Ilko Petkow
Standby Carpenter . . . . . . Christoph Baumstieger
Standby Painter . . . . Enzo Enzel

Sound Mixer . . . . Manfred Banach
Boom Operator . . . . Dirk Schäfer

SFX Supervisor . . . . Gerd Feuchter
SFX Foremen . . . . Till Hertrich
Rolf Hanke
SFX Technicians . . . . Gonzalo Ortega
Marcus Schmidt

Production Coordinators . . . . Susanne Fischer
Doris Edwards
Assistant Production
Coordinator . . . . Adam-Victor Linkowski

Construction Manager . . . . Dierk Grahlow
Assistant Construction
Manager . . . . Andre Brueggemann
HOD Painter . . . . Pablo Alza
Construction Department
Coordinator . . . . Nadin Meyer

Art Department Coordinator . . . . Robert Blasi
Conceptual Artist . . . . Axel Eichhorst

Graphic Artist . . . . Jan Jericho

Assistant Set Decorator . . . . Mark Fielk
Leadman . . . . Christoph Lanksch
Set Decoration Department
Coordinator . . . . Lisa Folkens
Set Decoration Buyers . . . . Sascha Strutz
Patrick Wiethoff
Set Decoration Foreman . . . . Markus Hasler
Set Decoration Head Painter . . . . Kadi Fast
Senior Set Dresser . . . . Klaus Eckmann
Theatre Plays/Stage Decors . . . . . . Ilona Vovchyk

Assistant Property Master . . . . . Matthias Haase
Standby Props . . . . Oliver Kuhlmann
Sebastian Hanusch
Armourer Swords . . . . Roman Spacil

Unit Publicist . . . . Kathryn Donovan
Still Photographer . . . . Reiner Bajo

Additional 2nd
Assistant Directors . . . . Lisa Hauss
Ronny Schröder
3rd Assistant Directors . . . . Christopher Poth
Janina Huettenrauch
Assistants to Mr. Emmerich . . . . Eva von Malotky
Marco Antonio Shepherd
Assistant to Mr. Franco . . . . Sabina Friedland
Production Assistants . . . . Suza Kohlstedt
Katrin Ewerlin
Rickie-Lee Roberts
Sibylle Schuster
Christina Degenhardt
Consultants . . . . Lisa Wilson
Laura Wilson
Stage Manager . . . . Gisela Emberger
Assistant Stage Managers . . . . Sven Jorden
Paul Wolf
Jerome Lippelt

Choreographer . . . . Gabriela Dumitrescu
Dancers . . . . Tjadke Biallowons
Dafne-Maria Fiedler
Alexander Flache
Antonia Gerke
Sophie Hichert
Lukas Hötzel
Johannes Keusch
Vera Kreyer
Stefanie Lanius
Urban Luig
Jasmin Mehling
Elisabeth Milarch
Robert Munzinger
Benjamin Plath
Erik Studte
Johann Jakob Wurster

Dialect Coach . . . . Brendan Gunn
Additional Casting (Germany) . . . . . . Simone Baer

Casting Consultant (USA) . . . . April Webster
Extras Casting . . . . Johanna Ragwitz
Anton Ludwig
Production Accountants . . . . Anne Ford
Paul Meyer-Gerlt
Assistant Accountants . . . . Christian Wöltche
Bettina Brenner
Mario Lindner
Johannes Schwerdt

Transportation Coordinator . . . . Martin Kuschan
Transportation Captain . . . . Florian Haeger
Transportation Co-Captain . . . . Axel Hübner

Post Production
Additional Editing by . . . . Christoph Strothjohann
Assistant Editor . . . . Michael Timmers
Post Production
Supervisor . . . . Christopher Berg

Supervising Sound Editor /
Re-Recording Mixer . . . . . Hubert Bartholomae
Sound Effects Editors . . . . Phillipp Sellier
Christoph von Schoenburg
Fritz Dosch
Dialogue Editor . . . . Pit Kuhlmann
Supervising ADR Editor . . . . Simon Price
Foley Artist . . . . Andi Schneider

Post Sound Services provided by . . . . Solid Sound
Munich, Germany

Voice Casting by . . . . Louis Elman
Abigail Barbier

Original Period Music
Composed by . . . . Claire van Kampen
Score Conducted & Orchestrated by . . James Brett
Orchestrations . . . . Marcus Trumpp
Adam Langston
Additional Music by . . . . Marcus Trumpp
Score Performed
by . . . . . . Deutsches Filmorchester Babelsberg
Cello . . . . Dave Eggar
Hurdy Gurdy . . . . Matthias Loibner
Solo Vocals . . . . Ana Maria Lombo
Orchestra Contractor . . . . Klaus-Peter Bayer
Music Recorded at . . . . Scoring Stage Babelsberg
Music Preparation . . . . Heiko Music
Vic Fraser
Score Mixer . . . . Michael Schubert
Pro Tools Operator . . . . Falko Duczmal

Digital Intermediate . . . ARRI Film & TV Services
Digital Colorist . . . . Florian Utsi Martin
Titles by . . . . . . Lutz Lemke & Matthias Brauner
Negative Cutter . . . . Andrea Vogenauer

Visual Effects and Digital
Environments created by Uncharted Territory
VFX Production Manager . . . . Stacey Weigert
VFX Project Manager . . . . Katharina Koepke

165

Cast & Crew

Compositing Supervisor . . . . Rony Soussan
VFX Art Director . . . . Greg Strasz
Modeling Lead / Lighting Lead . . .André Cantarel
Animation Lead. . . . . .Conrad Murrey
Lighting TDs . . . . Robert Freitag
Irfan Celik
Tom Freitag
Hannes Poser
Gereon Zwosta
Compositing Lead. . . . . .Ryan Smolarek
Senior Compositor . . . . Pieter Van Houte
Sequence Lead. . . . . Brian Fisher
Compositing TD . . . . Robert Zeltsch
Compositors . . . . Sandra Balej
Gregory Chalenko
Wing Kwok
Thomas Lautenbach

Compositors (cont.). . . . . Sebastian Schütt
Julia Smola
Caroline Weidenhiller
Lead Matte Painter. . . . . .René Borst
Matte Painter . . . . .Alp Altiner
Senior Texture Artist. . . . . Knuth Möde
Modeler . . . . Christine Toni Neumann
Modelers / Texture Painters. . . . Philip Hartmann
Martin Bohm
Massive TD . . . . .Timm Dapper
Senior Matchmove TD. . . . . .Denis Trutanic
Senior IT Manager . . . . .Jack Ghoulian
IT Manager . . . . .Tilo Meisel
VFX Coordinator . . . . Guido Medert
VFX Project Management
Assistant . . . . Dieter Primig
VFX Production Assistant . . . . Jakob Degen

Programmers. . . . . .Daniel König
Ulrik Schou Jørgensen
Marine Researcher. . . . . .Carsten Engel
VFX Data Wranglers . . . . Ante Dekovic
Jon Brown

Filmed at Studio Babelsberg
Potsdam, Germany

MUSIC

"Night of the Long Knives"
Written by Byrd & Hirschfelder
Performed by David Hirschfelder
Courtesy The Decca Music Group
Under licence from Universal
Music Operations Ltd.

Special Thanks to
The National Trust
Montacute House, Somerset

Prints by DELUXE®

Supported by

 AMERICAN HUMANE

A Co-Production among
ANONYMOUS PICTURES LIMITED,
VIERZEHNTE BABELSBERG FILM GmbH,
SIEBENTE BABELSBERG FILM GmbH
and
ACHTE BABELSBERG FILM GmbH

SONY
make.believe

COLUMBIA
PICTURES

Acknowledgments

The publisher wishes to thank the following for their support of this book:

For their generous editorial contributions to this book, much appreciation to Director Roland Emmerich for his wonderful introduction and enthusiasm for the project, to Screenwriter John Orloff for his insightful piece, and to Charles Beauclerk for his fascinating essay.

Also, special thanks for their exclusive contributions to this book: Theater Scenes Director Tamara Harvey, Costume Designer Lisy Christl, Production Designer Sebastian Krawinkel, Visual Effects Supervisors Volker Engel & Marc Weigert, and Director of Photography Anna J. Foerster. Also, appreciation for the wonderful photographs from Stills Photographer Reiner Bajo.

At Centropolis Entertainment for their enormous and kind help on this project: Kirstin Winkler, Marco Shepherd, Samantha Schwartz, Aaron Boyd, and especially Eva von Malotky, who skillfully collected and coordinated so many of the components for this book.

Many thanks to everyone at Sony Pictures Entertainment who assisted in providing assets and supervision for this project.

Noteworthy assistance from Matthew Bailey at the National Portrait Gallery in London, Marilyn Palmeri at the Morgan Library, and Alec Cobbe, who was so generous granting the use of his Shakespeare portrait. Also thanks for kind advice from documentarians Lisa Wilson and Laura Matthias.

At Night and Day Design: Many thanks to Designer Timothy Shaner for making the words and images more lovely than a summer's day, and to Writer Christopher Measom for his turn of phrase and attention to detail.

And the Newmarket Press team: Frank DeMaio, Keith Hollaman, especially Paul Sugarman for his extensive Shakespearean expertise, Heidi Sachner, Harry Burton, and Tracey Bussell.

—Esther Margolis, Publisher, Newmarket Press

Introduction "A Shakespearean Conspiracy" by Roland Emmerich © 2011 Roland Emmerich
"Shakespeare's Lost Kingdom" by Charles Beauclerk © 2011 Charles Beauclerk
"The Soul of the Script" by John Orloff © 2011 John Orloff

Page 24: portrait of Edward de Vere: Private collection; on loan to the National Portrait Gallery, London.
Page 26 and 27: portrait of William Cecil and portrait of Queen Elizabeth I: © National Portrait Gallery,
London. Page 29: The Cobbe Portrait of William Shakespeare, unknown artist c. 1610. Cobbe Collection,
reproduced by copyright held by a private trust.

FIRST EDITION
10 9 8 7 6 5 4 3 2 1

ISBN: 978-1-55704-975-9 (hardcover)
ISBN: 978-1-55704-992-6 (paperback)

Library of Congress Catalog-in-Publication Data available upon request.

QUANTITY PURCHASES
Companies, professional groups, clubs, and other organizations may qualify for special terms
when ordering quantities of this title. For information, email sales@newmarketpress.com or
write to Special Sales, Newmarket Press, 18 East 48th Street, New York, NY 10017;
call (212) 832-3575 ext. 19 or 1-800-669-3903; FAX (212) 832-3629;.

Manufactured in the United States of America

Special thanks to writer Christopher Measom and designer Timothy Shaner
at Night and Day Design (nightanddaydesign.biz).

Produced by Newmarket Press: Esther Margolis, President and Publisher; Frank DeMaio,
Production Director; Keith Hollaman, Executive Editor; Paul Sugarman, Digital Supervisor

Other Newmarket Pictorial Moviebooks and Newmarket Insider Film Books include:

Angels and Demons: The Illustrated Movie Companion
The Art of How to Train Your Dragon
The Art of Monsters vs. Aliens
The Art of X2*
The Art of X-Men: The Last Stand
Bram Stoker's Dracula: The Film and the Legend*
Chicago: The Movie and Lyrics*
Dances with Wolves: The Illustrated Story of the Epic Film*
E.T. The Extra-Terrestrial: From Concept to Classic*
Gladiator: The Making of the Ridley Scott Epic Film
*Good Night, and Good Luck: The Screenplay and
History Behind the Landmark Movie**

Hotel Rwanda: Bringing the True Story of an African Hero to Film*
The Jaws Log
Memoirs of a Geisha: A Portrait of the Film
Milk: A Pictorial History of Harvey Milk
The Mummy: Tomb of the Dragon Emperor
Ray: A Tribute to the Movie, the Music, and the Man*
Rush Hour 1, 2, 3: Lights, Camera, Action!
Saving Private Ryan: The Men, The Mission, The Movie
Schindler's List: Images of the Steven Spielberg Film
Superbad: The Illustrated Moviebook*
Tim Burton's Corpse Bride: An Invitation to the Wedding

*Includes the screenplay

www.newmarketpress.com